WELL

PRENTICE-HALL FOUNDATIONS OF MODERN LINGUISTICS SERIES

Sanford A. Schane
editor

John Kimball The Formal Theory of Grammar

Robert P. Stockwell Foundations of Syntactic Theory

Sanford A. Schane Generative Phonology

Theo Vennemann Introduction to Historical Linguistics

Maurice Gross Mathematical Models in Linguistics

William S-Y. Wang Phonetics

Janet Dean Fodor Semantics

Suzette Haden Elgin What Is Linguistics?

Other titles to be announced

Generative Phonology

SANFORD A. SCHANE

University of California, San Diego

PRENTICE-HALL, INC., Englewood Cliffs, New Jersey

Library of Congress Cataloging in Publication Data

SCHANE, SANFORD A
   Generative phonology.

   (Foundations of modern linguistics)
   Bibliography: p. 123
   1. Grammar, Comparative and general—Phonology.
2. Generative grammar. I. Title.
P217.S28   414   72–7268
ISBN 0–13–350967–2
ISBN 0–13–350959–1 (pbk.)

© 1973 PRENTICE-HALL, INC., Englewood Cliffs, New Jersey

Printed in the United States of America

10 9 8 7 6 5 4 3 2 1

PRENTICE-HALL INTERNATIONAL INC., LONDON
PRENTICE-HALL OF AUSTRALIA PTY. LTD., SYDNEY
PRENTICE-HALL OF CANADA, LTD., TORONTO
PRENTICE-HALL OF INDIA PRIVATE LIMITED, NEW DELHI
PRENTICE-HALL OF JAPAN, INC., TOKYO

To Morris Halle

Editor's Note

Language permeates human interaction, culture, behavior, and thought. The *Foundations of Modern Linguistics Series* focuses on current research in the nature of language.

Linguistics as a discipline has undergone radical change within the last decade. Questions raised by today's linguists are not necessarily those asked previously by traditional grammarians or by structural linguists. Most of the available introductory texts on linguistics, having been published several years ago, cannot be expected to portray the colorful contemporary scene. Nor is there a recent book surveying the spectrum of modern linguistic research, probably because the field is still moving too fast, and no one author can hope to capture the diverse moods reflected in the various areas of linguistic inquiry. But it does not seem unreasonable now to ask individual specialists to provide a picture of how they view their own particular field of interest. With the *Foundations of Modern Linguistics Series* we will attempt to organize the kaleidoscopic present-day scene. Teachers in search of up-to-date materials can choose individual volumes of the series for courses in linguistics and in the nature of language.

If linguistics is no longer what it was ten years ago its relation to other disciplines has also changed. Language is peculiarly human and it is found deep inside the mind. Consequently, the problems of modern linguistics are equally of concern to anthropology, sociology, psychology, and philosophy. Linguistics has always had a close affiliation with literature and with foreign language learning. Developments in other areas have had their impact on linguistics. There are mathematical models of language and formalisms of its structure. Computers are being used to test grammars. Other sophisticated instrumentation has revolutionized research in phonetics. Advances in neurology have contributed to our understanding of language pathologies and to the development of language. This series is also intended, then, to acquaint other disciplines with the progress going on in linguistics.

Finally, we return to our first statement. Language permeates our lives. We sincerely hope that the *Foundations of Modern Linguistics Series* will be of interest to anyone wanting to know what language is and how it affects us.

Sanford A. Schane, *editor*

Contents

Dynamic Phonology

Phonological Rules   *62*

Underlying Representations   *74*

Ordered Rules   *84*

Preface

Phonology is concerned with the sound structure of language; generative phonology is a theory of this structure. I hope that this book will satisfy the curiosity of those who have heard of phonology and want to know something about it. The theoretical framework underlying generative phonology owes its development primarily to Noam Chomsky and Morris Halle. The theory and its application to English are set forth in their monumental work, *The Sound Pattern of English*. It is also my desire, then, that my book provide the necessary foundation for anyone wanting to approach their work as well as other current phonological literature.

This book does not describe in great detail the phonological structure of any particular language. Rather, we shall be looking at the properties of phonological systems in general—what is common to the phonologies of all languages. Of course, general phonological theory cannot be divorced from what happens in specific languages, since the theory evolves from experience with real linguistic data. Therefore, when discussing theoretical points we will refer to examples from various languages. There happens to be a good deal of data from English and French. That many examples should be drawn from English is self-evident; the emphasis on French reflects my personal bias.

I have generally avoided polemics, for I thought it best to present one coherent view. Yet I have tried to point out those aspects of the theory which are inadequate or not too solid, and I hope not to give the impression that generative phonology is a *fait accompli*. In fact, phonology, like other areas of linguistics, is going through a period of flux.

In spoken language sound conveys meaning, and meaning is manifested through sound. Unfortunately, due to space limitation, I was unable to show how phonology fits into a total theory of language, how it is interrelated with the syntax and the semantics. Generative phonological theory has not evolved isolated from the rest of language, but has been part of a comprehensive theory of language known as transformational grammar. Two introductory books painting the whole picture are Langacker's *Language and its Structure* and Grinder and Elgin's *A Primer of Transformational Grammar*. A much more technical work is Chomsky's *Aspects of the Theory of Syntax*.

Language data and analyses are taken from various sources: Chomsky and Halle (English), Gleason (Chatino, Hanunoo, Turkish, Yoruba), Harris (Spanish), Hyman (Nupe), Koutsoudas (Russian), Kuroda (Yawelmani), Lee (Korean), Lightner (Russian), Stewart (Twi), Vennemann (German), and Walker (Diegueño). The French data are from my *French Phonology and Morphology*. The works of Hockett, Jakobson, Ladefoged, and Trubetzkoy were instrumental for examples of the different types of phonological patterns discussed in the second chapter. Complete references to all sources are in the Bibliography.

I am grateful to James Fidelholtz, James McCawley, Masayoshi Shibatani, Timothy Smith, and William S.-Y. Wang for comments on an earlier version of this work. Their criticisms were most helpful for subsequent revision. If I have not taken all of their suggestions into account, and the book suffers in parts, I alone am at fault. The Linguistic Department of the University of California at San Diego was most generous in providing material and human assistance.

Sanford A. Schane

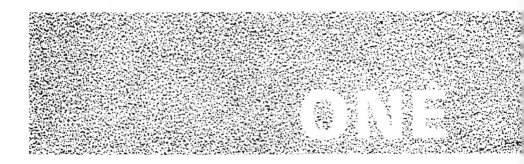

Segmental Phonology

The Segment

Suppose you were asked how many sounds there are in the spoken word *cat*. For the sake of the discussion let us hope your answer is three. Yet X-ray films of speech as well as spectrograms (voice prints of the acoustic properties of speech) show that speech sounds are not produced as a series of discrete segments, but rather that sounds merge and blend into one another. In pronouncing *cat*, during the articulation of the initial consonant the tongue is already anticipating the articulation of the following vowel. From such records it is often impossible to determine exactly where one sound ends and the next begins. This leads to an interesting paradox. Although a speech signal may be physically *continuous*, we seem to perceive it as a sequence of *discrete* entities.

That utterances can be represented as a sequence of discrete units is one of the basic theoretical assumptions of phonology. Because of this assumption we are able to talk about individual segments and sequences of segments, and to develop a notation in which we employ discrete symbols for representing utterances. In fact, it is difficult to conceive of any kind of phonological description (or scientific description, for that matter) being made without postulating discrete units. But do we really have a right to claim that speech is segmentable if the articulatory and acoustic aspects suggest the opposite? Or is the discrete nature of speech an artifact of analysis, something invented by the linguist in order to describe language?

There is evidence that speakers also conceive of utterances as composed of discrete entities. Earlier we suggested that *cat* is composed of three sounds. You might say that speakers are influenced by the written language, in which *cat* is spelled with three letters. But alphabetic writing can in fact be used as one argument in favor of the segmental view of speech, since with such writing systems there is a correlation between a sequence of graphic symbols and a purported sequence of speech sounds. The fit may not always be ideal but it is undeniable that there is a correlation. By the same token, a phonetician or linguistic field worker confronted with an unknown language can immediately begin to transcribe with alphabetic symbols what he hears spoken. Fromkin has shown that "slips of the tongue" provide another kind of evidence for the reality of segments, particularly spoonerisms such as *with this wing I thee red* or *Homsky and Challe*, where what we are calling individual segments have been interchanged. Rhymes, such as *the fat cat in the hat*, also suggest the need for recognizing individual segments, and not only by children. (These observations do not imply that speakers may not also perceive larger phonological units, such as the syllable.)

How do we reconcile our view that linguists require segments to analyze language and that speakers and listeners psychologically "feel" that speech is segmentable, with the articulatory and acoustic facts which show speech as continuous? Let us first consider the speaker. Assume that he intends to utter a sequence of discrete sounds and then instructs his vocal apparatus to produce this discrete sequence. However, the vocal apparatus is constructed in such a way that in executing the command it does not produce one sound, stop, produce the next one, stop, and so on, but instead functions continually in motion, moving from one sound to the next and even preparing for sounds in advance, a much more efficient way to operate. If we adopt this view, then the transitions from one sound to the next—the slurrings and blurrings—become automatic features of the vocal mechanism and as such can remain outside the actual intention of the speaker.

Now what about the listener? If the speech signal is continuous, why should he perceive it as discontinuous? Probably because that is the only way the mind can organize language. We know that humans do perceive continuous phenomena as though discontinuous. Consider writing. The written word ᴄɑƚ is a continuum, yet we perceive it as containing three discrete letters, just as printed *cat* does. In language the perceptual, the subjective, the discrete take precedence over the physical, the objective, the continuous. This discrepancy incidentally supplies interesting fuel for the philosophical controversy of appearance versus reality.

It's What You "Think" that Counts

X-rays and spectrograms show not only that speech is physically continuous, but also that no two utterances—even occurrences of what is supposed to be the "same" utterance—are exactly identical. If two persons say *tea for two*, individual anatomical differences in the shapes of their vocal tracts will cause the respective acoustic records of this utterance to differ. Such individual differences are responsible for personal voice quality, which, for example, helps us to recognize a familiar voice on a dark night. But even the same individual will not articulate the same thing the same way each time. You would normally round your lips for the vowel of *two* but the amount of lip rounding could vary from one time to the next. In saying *tea for two* you might at one time have gum in your mouth, or be whispering it as a "sweet nothing" on another occasion. In spite of all the minute and even not so minute differences which an accurate acoustic record might show, we nonetheless perceive the various occurrences of *tea for two* as being the "same" utterance. In fact, we could "do" no linguistics (nor would language even be possible) if we were never able to assert that two utterances are identical. So here is another case where what we perceive does not correlate with what is physically so.

We are interested only in those phonetic differences which are "linguistically significant." Let us try to clarify this notion of linguistic significance. Some phonetic differences serve to differentiate forms. The words *p*in, *b*in, *t*in, *d*in, *k*in, *f*in, *s*in, and *w*in differ only in their initial consonant segments. Similarly, the words b*ea*t, b*i*t, b*ai*t, b*e*t, b*a*t, b*oo*t, b*oa*t, and b*ough*t differ only in their vowel segments. Segments whose function is to contrast forms have traditionally been called *phonemes*. So, to begin with, we can say that phonetic differences which are phonemic are linguistically significant.

But a phoneme is not necessarily phonetically invariant. For example, *p* occurs as the first segment in *p*in, as the second segment in s*p*in, and as the last segment in ni*p*. Although these are all occurrences of the same phoneme *p*, consideration of the actual articulatory implementations of this phoneme—its pronunciations—reveals that it has different *phonetic variants* or *allophones*. The initial *p* of *p*in is phonetically aspirated—it is produced with a puff of air. The *p* of s*p*in, on the other hand, has no aspiration. This same phonetic difference holds for *t* and *k*; compare *t*an with S*t*an and *k*in with s*k*in. With final *p*, *t*, and *k*, the situation is variable. In ni*p*, ni*t*, and nic*k*, the final consonant may be either aspirated or unaspirated. This variation is stylistic, final aspiration generally being associated with formal style or affectation. So a phoneme may have several allophones (such as aspirated and unaspirated *p*), and these allophonic differences are also linguistically significant.

Linguistically significant phonetic differences are those which characterize native control of a language. For example, failure to distinguish *pit* and *bit* would be un-English. It would be un-English for initial *p*, *t*, *k* to be unaspirated (but would be excellent French or Spanish). It is English for aspiration to be variable at the end of a word, since there are recognized social styles and dialects of English. But it is *not* peculiar to English to have the voice range of a tenor or soprano, to mumble in one's beard, or to talk with a mouth full of spinach. Nor is it a part of English for the same speaker to aspirate initial *p, t, k* with the identical amount of physical force each time. Interestingly enough, it is not even necessary that some measurable accepted range of aspiration occur with these initial segments. The only thing linguistically significant is that aspiration be "perceived." For example, a speaker at a lively cocktail party may have aspirated, but the aspiration was masked by the surrounding noise. What is important is whether the listener "thought" he heard aspiration, whether he perceived the utterance as a perfectly normal English one. By now it should come as no surprise that perception need not always jibe with the actual articulation or with the acoustic signal.

How Abstract Is Abstract?

The distinction between phonemes and allophones allows us to recognize two levels of phonological representation—the level of pronunciation or what has traditionally been referred to as the *phonetic* level, and the level of contrast or opposition, the *phonemic*.

It is important to realize that what we are calling a phonetic representation is not a representation of the physical phonetics—neither a record of the articulatory mechanism in motion nor of an acoustic signal. It is a representation in which speech is viewed as a sequence of discrete segments which may differ from one another only in a limited number of ways. A phonetic representation for a particular language indicates the variation which is part of the recognized allophonic norms, so the phonetic level is already a significant abstraction from physical phonetics. It is traditional to use square brackets for indicating phonetic representations. Thus *pit* and *spit* would be phonetically transcribed [pʰit], [spit] or [pʰitʰ], [spitʰ], depending on the absence or presence of final aspiration. In generative phonology these representations are called *systematic phonetic*.

If a systematic phonetic representation is more abstract than a physical phonetic record, a phonemic representation is still more abstract, as even less phonetic detail is indicated. Phonemic representations are enclosed between diagonal bars. Hence, *pit* and *spit* are transcribed as /pit/ and /spit/. It is the phonemic representation which explicitly shows (since the same symbol is used) that what may be different at the systematic phonetic level—for example, the first segment of [pʰit] and the second segment of [spit]—are "sames" at this higher, more abstract level. The phonemic representations are related to the systematic phonetic by rules, such as the rules stating that /p/, /t/, /k/ are realized as phonetically aspirated [pʰ], [tʰ], [kʰ] in certain contexts.

Incidentally, when spelling reformists assail the English standard orthography for not being "phonetic" enough, or when educators cry out for "phonics" in teaching reading, and both align forces in favor of a system with a one-to-one correspondence between "sound" and "letter," what they really mean is phoneme and letter. There are few serious (?) spelling reformers demanding, for example, special symbols for indicating phonetically aspirated consonants.

The emphasis of American phonology in the 1940's and 1950's was on phonemics. Elaborate procedures were formulated for segmenting utterances and for discovering the phonemes of different languages. One of the outgrowths of generative phonology was a rejection of a phonemic level. It is not that generative phonologists denied a level more abstract than the systematic phonetic one, but rather that the phonemic level was not the right one. It was not abstract enough; it was still too close to the phonetic ground.

Consider the phonemic representations of the related forms *electric* and *electricity*—/elektrik/, /elektrisiti/. The stem final consonant has the variant realizations /k/ and /s/, the latter occurring before suffixes beginning with /i/. Just as we were able to say that in English the [pʰ] of *pit* and the [p] of *spit* can be represented at some higher level as a unique segment /p/, we would like to be able to say that the /k/ of *electric* and the /s/ of *electricity* are also, at a more abstract level of analysis, manifestations of some unique segment—let us say *k*. Then we could have abstract type representations such as |elektrik| and |elektrik + iti| (where the + shows the division between the stem and the suffix). These representations explicitly show that what we consider to be the same stem has the same representation. However, whereas in phonemic theory we could say that [pʰ] and [p] were variants of a single phoneme /p/, we cannot within that theory similarly group *k* and *s* as variants of a unique phoneme, precisely because /k/ and /s/ are independently recognized as phonemes of English. Hence, transcriptions such as |elektrik + iti| are not phonemic (and obviously not systematic phonetic) but represent a higher level of abstraction. Within generative phonology such representations are known as *systematic phonemic*, in contrast to the traditional phonemic type which generative phonologists have renamed *taxonomic* or *autonomous phonemic*. (Notice that English orthography also makes use of systematic phonemic spellings—*electric*, *electricity*, where unique *c* represents both variants.)

For the moment we will not become further embroiled in the controversy of systematic phonemic versus taxonomic phonemic representations. Both approaches recognize at least two levels of phonological representation—a level of pronunciation, the systematic phonetic, and a more abstract level where phonetic variance is reduced. The big question to which we return in a later chapter is: How abstract is abstract?

Phonological Patterns

The Search for a Universal Phonetics

There are at least three different goals we could demand of a phonetic theory. It must account for: (A) any kind of "noise" which the human vocal apparatus is capable of producing; (B) a subset of (A)—only those "sounds" which are linguistically significant in some language or other; (C) a subset of (B)—only those "sounds" which are linguistically significant in a particular language. A phonetic theory whose goal is set at (A) is not restricted enough, for such a theory would also describe grunts and groans, hysterical laughter and sobs, burps and belches—sounds which may have social repercussions but which are not linguistically significant in the sense discussed previously. A phonetic theory is overly powerful if it has to accommodate sounds which never occur as phonological entities in any human language. On the other hand, (C) is much too restrictive. By setting our goals at (C) we could have, for example, a phonetic theory of English, but such a model would not be applicable to any other language.

The only reasonable goal for a universal phonetics is (B)—a description of just those sounds which can be linguistically significant in some human language. By setting our goal at (B) we explicitly exclude myriad human "noises" which never play a role in language. Although (B) allows the description of many more sounds than are ever required for a particular language, it still makes the interesting claim that any human language can draw its sounds only from this "universal" inventory. Now consider this claim from the point of view of a child learning language. We know that an adult speaker has at his command only a small repertoire of the sound types of (B). Yet, at least at one time, all of (B) was "potentially" available to him. The child learning his first language or languages has no way of "knowing" whether he will hear Japanese or Russian or English or Hungarian. But given that the vocal mechanism is the same for all human beings, he has the potential for producing any of the sounds of (B). His task is to select eventually, from (B), just those sounds required for the language or languages he will be speaking. Only by having (B) as our phonetic theory are we able to compare different languages—to see how they are alike and how they differ in their phonetics and their phonological structure. What follows is to be viewed not as a detailed discussion of phonetics but as a minimum foundation for approaching phonology.

The First Split

The *vowel-consonant* dichotomy is intuitively the most basic division for phonetic classification. If we imagine articulation as being a series of openings and closings of the vocal tract, we can view vowels as constituting open stages where the outgoing air flows freely, and consonants, with their various degrees of constriction, as constituting more closed phases, where the outgoing air is impeded.

Perceptually, vowels are more audible than consonants; they carry the intonational features of stress and pitch, and they are the most "musical" of the sounds. (In singing, for example, it is the vowels which are prolonged.) The vowel is the nucleus of the syllable. Most of the time, a syllable contains a vowel with or without one or more surrounding consonants. We say "most of the time" because, ironically, the syllable as a unit has not been 100 per cent satisfactorily defined, but that it plays a role in many kinds of phonological processes is undeniable.

VOWELS

The Basic Series

PAPA, PIPI, AND PUPU

It is traditional to classify vowels according to the position of the tongue and shape of the lips. If we consider just the three vowels *i* (as in mach*i*ne), *u* (as in r*u*de), and *a* (as in f*a*ther), we observe (for example, by inserting a finger into the mouth as the various vowel sounds are made) that for *i* the body of the tongue bunches up *high* in the *front* part of the mouth close to the hard palate, whereas for *u* the tongue bunches up *high* in the *back* part of the mouth close to the soft palate or *velum*. Furthermore, for *i* the lips are spread or *unrounded*, whereas for *u* they are *rounded*. In the case of *a*, the tongue is relatively flat or *low* in the back part of the mouth, with no lip rounding. These positions can be represented schematically:

	Front Unrounded	Back Unrounded	Back Rounded
High	i		u
Low		a	

The vowels *i*, *a*, and *u*, found in practically all languages, are so common that we shall refer to them as the *basic three-vowel pattern*. Some languages having only these three as vowel phonemes* are Eskimo and some Arabic dialects. In Russian only *i*, *a*, and *u* occur in unstressed syllables.

Jakobson has claimed that *i*, *a*, and *u* universally are the first vowel phonemes to appear in the speech of children—witness *papa, mama, dada, kaka, pipi, pupu*. Why should these be the most basic, occurring as segments in nearly all languages and as the first in child language? Note that they are maximally opposed one from the other. Thus, *a* as a low vowel is opposed to *i* and *u* as high vowels. Perceptually, *i* and *u* are opposed to each other in pitch. The tongue frontness and lip spreading for *i* result in a small cavity between tongue and lips with no constriction at the lips. This configuration produces a high-pitched vowel. Conversely, due to the rounded lips and backed tongue for *u* there is a narrowed aperture at the lips and a large cavity between lips and tongue. The result is a low-pitched vowel. (If you whisper the vowels, so that their inherent pitch is not masked by vocal cord vibrations, you can determine that *i* has the highest pitch, *u* the lowest, and *a* is somewhere in between.)

All other vowels are located within the perceptual space bounded by *i*, *a*, and *u*. Naturally, for each new vowel added, the perceptual distance between adjacent vowels decreases. Hence, children and the languages of the world first select those vowels which are maximally different.

THE MIDS AND THE LOWS

One of the most common vowel systems is composed of five vowels: the three basic ones plus two others which are intermediate in height between high and low, but are opposed to each other in the same way as *i* and *u*—mid front unrounded *e* (as in pr*e*y) and mid back rounded *o* (as in r*o*se).

---

*In this chapter "phonemic" refers to taxonomic phonemic.

	Front Unrounded	Back Unrounded	Back Rounded
High	i		u
Mid	e		o
Low		a	

Some languages having this five-vowel pattern are Spanish, Latin, Czech, Polish, modern Greek, Japanese, and Hawaiian.

A seven-vowel system can be formed by adding to the five-vowel pattern a pair of low vowels—front unrounded æ (as in c*a*t) and back rounded ɔ (as in b*ou*ght).

	Front Unrounded	Back Unrounded	Back Rounded
High	i		u
Mid	e		o
Low	æ	a	ɔ

A variant of the seven-vowel pattern has the vowel ɛ (as in p*e*t) instead of æ. Italian and Vulgar Latin exemplify this system.

The Mixed Series

In addition to the two basic vowel series, front unrounded and back rounded, there may be *mixed* vowels: either *front rounded* or *back unrounded*. One type of mixed system is the five-vowel pattern with a series of front rounded vowels; high *ü* (as in French t*u* or German *ü*ber) and mid *ö* (as in French p*eu* or German m*ö*gen). (Front rounded vowels can be produced by saying the corresponding front unrounded vowel, then rounding the lips without moving the tongue.)

	Front Unrounded	Front Rounded	Back Unrounded	Back Rounded
High	i	ü		u
Mid	e	ö		o
Low			a	

German, various Dutch dialects, Hungarian, and some dialects of French have this vowel system.

There is also the seven-vowel pattern with a series of front rounded vowels: high *ü*, mid *ö*, and low *œ* (as in French p*eu*r). Standard French has this system.

	Front Unrounded	Front Rounded	Back Unrounded	Back Rounded
High	i	ü		u
Mid	e	ö		o
Low	ɛ	œ	a	ɔ

The *back unrounded* vowels, in addition to *a*, are high *ɨ* (as in ros*e*s) and mid ʌ (as in b*u*t).

Rumanian has seven vowels—the five-vowel system with the two additional back unrounded vowels.

	Front Unrounded	Back Unrounded	Back Rounded
High	i	ɨ	u
Mid	e	ʌ	o
Low		a	

Are There Only Front and Back Vowels?

The phonetics literature sometimes mentions central (between front and back) unrounded vowels, and *a* is not infrequently referred to as such a vowel. Central vowels are perceptually similar to back unrounded ones. Although there is a phonetic difference between the two types, languages rarely exploit this difference as a means for differentiating vowel phonemes, so that central and back unrounded do not *generally* contrast (although Swedish is reported to have such a contrast).

For classificatory purposes we will recognize only two degrees of backness: *front* or *back*. Combining these with two states of rounding and three degrees of vowel height, we arrive at a pattern with a maximum of 12 vowels. Probably no language has all of these as separate phonemes.

	Front		Back	
	Unrounded	Rounded	Unrounded	Rounded
High	i	ü	ɨ	u
Mid	e	ö	ʌ	o
Low	æ	œ	a	ɔ

Are There Only Three Vowel Heights?

English has five front unrounded vowels, exemplified in b*ea*t, b*i*t, b*ai*t, b*e*t, b*a*t. This is not really a system with five vowel heights, because the English vowels can be further classified as *tense* or *lax*. Where tense and lax vowels contrast in the following chart, a diacritic over the vowel serves to differentiate the two types. The high and mid tense vowels are represented phonetically as diphthongs (see p. 19), hence the *y* and *w* in the transcriptions.

Front unrounded
	High	īy (b*ea*t)	ĭ (b*i*t)
	Mid	ēy (b*ai*t)	ĕ (b*e*t)
	Low		æ (b*a*t)

Back rounded
	High	ūw (b*oo*t)	ŭ (b*oo*k)
	Mid	ōw (b*oa*t)	
	Low	ɔ̄ (b*ou*ght)	

Back unrounded
	High		ɨ (ros*e*s)
	Mid		ʌ (b*u*t) or ə (sof*a*)
	Low	ā (f*a*ther)	

There are at least three good arguments demonstrating that English has three vowel heights with tense and lax vowels rather than five vowel heights. First, there are articulatory differences between the so-called tense and lax vowels. Tense vowels are produced with greater muscular tension, they are maintained longer, and the articulatory organs deviate more from the rest position in their formation. (The differences in muscular tension can be verified by pressing the fingers against the throat while uttering tense and lax vowels.) From a perceptual point of view, tense vowels are more distinct. Next, there is an interesting distributional constraint on lax vowels. When stressed they appear only in a closed syllable (followed by one or more consonants). Stressed tense vowels, on the other hand, occur in both open and closed syllables.

b*ee*		b*ay*		b*oo*	
b*ea*t	b*i*t	b*ai*t	b*e*t	b*oo*t	b*oo*k

Finally, there are phonological alternations between pairs of tense and lax vowels (although not of the same height): s*a*ne, s*a*nity; obsc*e*ne, obsc*e*nity; red*u*ce, red*u*ction.

German is another language with three vowel heights and pairs of tense-lax vowels. Twi, a West African language, also has both types. So it would appear that three vowel heights are all that ever need to be recognized. However, Kiparsky cites a Swiss German dialect with four front unrounded vowels which he calls a four-height system, as there is no evidence in support of any tense-lax distinction. In any case, if there are vowel systems with more than three heights, they are rare.

Among the lax vowels ə, called *schwa*, has a special status. It is also referred to as the "reduced" vowel since it so often alternates with various "full" vowels. Thus, in the related words *photograph* [fōwtəgræf and *photography* [fetāgrəfïy], the stressed vowels in the first and third syllables of *photograph* alternate with unstressed schwas in the same positions in *photography*; conversely, the full vowel in the second syllable of *photography* is in alternation with the reduced vowel in the second syllable of *photograph*. The schwa also occurs in German—for example, the final vowel of *bitte*. Many languages have only a single lax vowel in the system, which is then the schwa. This is the situation in French, where all vowels are tense except for the schwa. An example of the French schwa is the first vowel of *petit*.

Prosodic Elements

Stress, *pitch*, and *length* are prosodic elements usually associated with the syllable, and most often with a particular vowel.

Stress, impressionistically, is associated with increased loudness. In English, grammatical differences can be signaled by the placement of primary stress. The word *survey* as a verb is stressed on the second syllable, but as a noun on the first. Compound nouns and noun phrases, such as *blackbird* and *black bird*, also exemplify stress differences. We have already seen how, for words such as *photograph* and *photography*, stress conditions the occurrence of full and of reduced vowels.

In English we are familiar with pitch as it pertains to *intonation*. The same sequence of words may have different connotations depending on the pitch contours, so that *You're coming!* uttered with a falling intonation—a command —means something different from the same sequence with a rising contour, *You're coming?*—a question. On the other hand, many languages of Southeast Asia, Africa, and America are *tone* languages in which each syllable has associated with it a particular pitch level (high, mid, low, falling, rising, and so on). Words can be minimally differentiated through tones. In Thai, the sequence *maa* with a high tone means 'horse', with a mid tone 'come', and with a rising tone 'dog'. Thus $\overline{maa}$ *maa* means 'the horse comes' whereas *mǎa maa* means 'the dog comes'.

Perceptually, the prosodic feature of length is timing. In English a vowel is phonetically longer before a voiced consonant (see p. 21) than before a voiceless one—be*a*d, be*a*t, and b*a*g, b*a*ck. These differences are never phonemic, as the length is entirely due to the consonantal environment. Phonemic vowel length did exist in Latin—port*a* 'door' (nominative singular), versus *porta*: (ablative singular). At times it may be useful to analyze a phonetically long segment as a sequence of two identical short ones, which are then called a *geminate*. (Note the Thai example on p. 14.)

CONSONANTS

Place of Articulation

The consonants *p*, *t*, and *k* are among the most basic; they are part of the consonant systems of nearly all languages. These three are also among the first to emerge in children's speech—notice nursery forms such as *papa, pipi, tata, kaka, kuku*. Radically different articulations are involved for each of these consonants. The *labial p* is formed at the lips, the *dental t* is made with the blade of the tongue (front part including tip) in contact with the region of the upper teeth, while the *velar k* is made with the body of the tongue against the velum (soft palate).

In *Sound Pattern of English* two parameters—*anterior* and *coronal*—are used for classifying these consonants. Anterior sounds, such as *p* and *t*, are formed at the extreme forward part of the mouth, from the lips to the alveolar (upper gum) ridge; hence, they are opposed to nonanterior sounds such as *k* articulated further back. Coronal sounds are made with the blade of the tongue; thus, coronal *t* is opposed to noncoronal *p* and *k*.

Anterior and/or Coronal Articulations

Among the labial consonants, the phonetics literature frequently distinguishes between *bilabials—p, b, m,*—made with both lips, and *labiodentals—f, v*—made with the lower lip against the upper teeth. Another distinction is between *dentals* proper and *alveolars*. In French and Spanish, *t, d, n* involve contact at the teeth, whereas English *t, d, n* are made against the *alveolar* ridge, the gum region behind the teeth. Rarely, both types may be in phonemic contrast, as in Malayalam, a language of India. Other dental consonants include English θ (as in *th*in) and ð (as in *th*en). In most languages *s* and *z* are alveolars.

The tongue tip can be retracted—anywhere from just behind the alveolar ridge to the roof of the palate—to produce the so-called *retroflex* consonants, which occur in Swedish, many of the languages of India, and some American

Indian languages. The English *r*, as in *r*ed, phonetically is often a type of retroflex consonant. However, as a post-alveolar articulation, retroflex consonants are somewhat rare. Much more common are the *palato-alveolars*, where the blade of the tongue makes contact in the area extending from the alveolar region to the hard palate. English has four palato-alveolars: č (as in *ch*air), ǰ (as in *j*udge), š (as in *sh*e), ž (as in vi*s*ion). As the palato-alveolars are not made exclusively in the extreme forward part of the mouth, they, like velars, are nonanterior. However, as the blade of the tongue is involved in the articulation, they share with the dentals (and alveolars) the trait of being coronal.

NONANTERIOR AND NONCORONAL

Velar consonants such as *k*, *g*, ŋ (as in lo*ng*) are articulated in the same region as the vowel *u*. Hence, for velars the *body of the tongue* is *high* and *back*. There are also *palatal* consonants in which the body of the tongue is *high* and *front*, as for *i*. English *y* is a palatal consonant. The body of the tongue can be retracted beyond the velar region so that the constriction is in the area of the uvula, the hanging appendage at the end of the velum. English has no consonants of the *uvular* type. In French and German, the "*r*-sound" is frequently uvular (if it is not a tongue-tip trill, as in Spanish or Italian). The uvular *r* impressionistically is the "gargling" *r* made in the throat. The most posterior lingual articulation is in the region of the pharynx—the body of the tongue is retracted toward the back of the throat. *Pharyngeal* consonants are rare, the language best known for them being Arabic.

Manner of Articulation

Consonants require a certain degree of constriction in the vocal tract—either total occlusion or a narrowing exceeding that found in the high vowels. It is these different degrees of closure which are known as *manners of articulation*.

STOPS

Stops, or plosives, are made with total occlusion in the oral cavity and with the velum raised so that no air escapes through the nasal passage. As a consequence, pressure is built up behind the point of articulation. When the occlusion is released one perceives the "popping" sound characteristic of stops. There are six stops in English: the labials, *p* and *b*; the dentals (actually alveolars), *t* and *d*; and the velars, *k* and *g*. All languages have stops, and nearly all languages have stops in the labial, dental, and velar regions. (Some Iroquoian languages lack labials, and there are Polynesian languages in which either dentals or velars are lacking.) Many languages have only these three stop positions—for example, English, French, Spanish, and German. (We shall illustrate with only one consonant from each place of articulation.)

Labial	Dental	Velar
p	t	k

A language may have one or more stops in addition to the three basic ones. Hungarian has a palato-alveolar series, often called palatal.

Labial	Dental	Palato-alveolar	Velar
p	t	c	k

Malayalam has contrasts among dental, alveolar, and retroflex stops. Eskimo has a uvular stop which contrasts with its velar.

FRICATIVES

Fricatives, or continuants, involve extreme narrowing allowing only a small opening for the air stream to pass through (similar to what happens when a window is not securely shut). This leads to the characteristic "hissing" noise associated with these sounds. The most common fricative is the alveolar *s*; the occurrence of *s* is nearly universal. Also quite common are labial and palato-alveolar fricatives. French has these three as fricative phonemes.

Labial	Alveolar	Palato-alveolar
f	s	š

German has these three plus a velar fricative *x* (as in a*ch*).

Labial	Alveolar	Palato-alveolar	Velar
f	s	š	x

English has a dental θ in addition to the alveolar *s*, but no *x*.

Labial	Dental	Alveolar	Palato-alveolar
f	θ	s	š

Castilian Spanish also has a dental fricative, and a uvular X (the jota), but no palato-alveolar one.

Labial	Dental	Alveolar	Uvular
f	θ	s	X

Fricatives at other places of articulation are less common. Bilabial fricatives occur. In Ewe, an African language, bilabial ϕ, β, and labio-dental f, v are in contrast. Spanish has a phonetic bilabial fricative, which is an allophone of b occurring between vowels (as in ha*ber* [aβɛr]). German has a phonetic palatal fricative ς which is an allophone of x occurring contiguous to a front vowel (as in i*ch*). Uvular and pharyngeal fricatives are found in Arabic.

Some fricatives are more audible and hence perceptually "noisier" than others; they are *strident*. For all fricatives the air is forced through a narrow opening, but in the case of the strident ones it is directed against the upper teeth or the uvula. Thus, f, s, $\check{s}$, and X are strident fricatives, whereas ϕ, θ, ς, and x are nonstrident.

AFFRICATES

Affricates share properties with both stops and fricatives. Initially there is total occlusion, but, unlike stops, the occlusion is not instantaneously released; instead it is released with frication. In English, there are two affricates: palato-alveolar $\check{c}$ and $\check{j}$. Not all languages have affricates. French lacks them, for example. Many languages have only a single place of articulation for affricates, often the palato-alveolar, as in English or Spanish. German has no $\check{c}$ but has two other affricates: the labial p^f (as in *Pferd*) and the alveolar t^s (as in *zehn*). The fricative release of an affricate is almost always strident. However, in Chipeweyan, there is a contrast between a dental t^θ and an alveolar t^s. In any case, an affricate with a nonstrident release is exceedingly rare.

NASALS

Nasals, like stops, are produced with total occlusion but with a lowered velum, so that the air stream is free to pass through the nasal passage. The labial and the dental (or alveolar) nasals are probably universal. Many languages have, in addition, either a velar or a palato-alveolar (or palatal), as in Spanish *mañana*. English and German have the velar in their nasal systems.

Labial	Dental	Velar
m	n	ŋ

Spanish, French, and Italian exemplify the pattern with a palato-alveolar.

Labial	Dental	Palato-alveolar
m	n	ñ

LIQUIDS

Liquids include the *l* and *r* sounds, the *lateral* and the *nonlateral* liquids, respectively. For the laterals, the tongue effects total occlusion (just as it does for stops and nasals), but either one or both sides of it are lowered, allowing the air to escape through the mouth. Nearly all languages have a dental (or alveolar) *l*. A palato-alveolar λ, often called palatal *l*, is found in Italian (as in *figlia*) and in some Spanish and French dialects. (In other dialects, this sound has been replaced by *y*.)

The nonlateral liquids are the various *r*-sounds. Typically, they are made with the tip of the tongue in the dental or alveolar region, either as a *trill* or as a *flap*. For the trill, the tongue tip is set in vibration by the outgoing air stream, making several taps against the upper place of articulation. Spanish and Italian have trilled *r*'s. Some dialects of French and German also have the trill; however, other dialects, particularly the prestigious ones, have instead the uvular *r*, made by vibrating the uvula. For the *flap*, the tongue tip is quickly thrown once against the upper place of articulation. Spanish has a flap *r*, which contrasts with its trill—pe*r*o 'but' versus pe*rr*o 'dog'. A flap—called flap *D*—occurs phonetically in many dialects of American English as an allophone of a medial *t* or *d* in words such as *butter* or *ladder*, although in English this sound functions as a dental stop.

Many of the Oriental languages have a single liquid phoneme. In Japanese it is *r*. In Korean the liquid is realized as *r* before vowels, and as *l* elsewhere. A few African and American Indian languages have no liquid at all.

GLIDES: SEMIVOWELS

Semivowels, as the name indicates, are consonants which are vowel-like. They are produced with the body of the tongue in the same position in which high vowels are made, except that the tongue is closer to the palate. It is this extra narrowing which makes them consonants. Languages frequently have semivowels corresponding to one or more of their high vowels. English has the palatal (front unrounded) semivowel *y* (corresponding to *i*) and the labio-velar (back rounded) semivowel *w* (corresponding to *u*). French has three semivowels corresponding to the high vowels *i*, *ü*, and *u*.

Front Unrounded	Front Rounded	Back Rounded
y	ẅ	w

In many languages semivowels are always allophones of high vowels when next to another vowel.

A combination of vowel and semivowel may constitute a *diphthong*, which functions like a single vowel. English has the diphthongs *āy*, *ōy*, *āw*, and *yū*(*w*), as in *sigh*, *soy*, *sow*, and *few*. In most dialects of English the high and mid tense vowels *phonetically* are diphthongs: *īy*, *ēy*, *ūw*, *ōw*. Whether a sequence of vowel and semivowel functions as a diphthong depends on the structure of the language. In English, the semivowel and vowel of *yes* is not considered a diphthong. However, the similar sequence in Spanish, as in *siento* [syεnto] 'I feel', is considered a diphthong; it alternates with a simple vowel: *sentir* 'to feel'.

LARYNGEAL GLIDES

The laryngeal glides are *h* (as in *h*e) and *ʔ* (*glottal stop*). The *h* is usually described as a voiceless version (no vocal cord vibration) of the following sound. To produce a glottal stop, the larynx is tightly closed, by bringing the vocal cords together; when the glottis is opened a popping noise is heard. (Some phonetics manuals classify *ʔ* as a stop [hence the name glottal stop] and *h* as a fricative.) The glottal stop occurs phonetically in some types of New York English where it replaces *t* in words such as *bottle*. For practically all English speakers a glottal stop separates the two identical vowel sounds of the exclamation *uh-uh*, meaning "no". Of the two laryngeal glides, only *h* is phonemic in English. Quite a few American Indian languages have *ʔ* as a phoneme. Russian and Italian, on the other hand, have no laryngeal glide.

Sonorant versus Obstruent

Vowel-consonant is not the only major division of segments. Sounds are frequently classified according to their resonance properties—whether they are *sonorants* or *obstruents*.

Sonorants	Obstruents
Vowels	Stops
Nasals	Fricatives
Liquids	Affricates
Semivowels	Laryngeal glides

Among the consonants, the sonorants are the more vowel-like, the more musical-like. (In singing, sonorants are used to track a melody: for example, *la-la-la*, or *m-m-m*, or even *ya-ya-ya*, as in rock music; obstruents are rarely employed in this way except to imitate percussion instruments: *tum-tum-tum*.) Sonorants may function as syllabic peaks whenever these are not occupied by vowels. *Syllabic* nasals and liquids occur phonetically in English in unstressed position, particularly in final syllables, in words such as bott*om*, butt*on*, cyc*le*, butt*er*. (A syllabic semivowel would be a high vowel.) In Twi, both vowels and sonorant consonants can carry tone.

When *voicing* differences (presence or absence of vocal cord vibration) are contrastive, they almost always accompany the obstruents. This is the situation in English, where all stops, fricatives, and affricates come in voiceless and voiced pairs: *p*, *b*; *t*, *d*; *k*, *g*; *f*, *v*; *θ*, *ð*; *s*, *z*; *š*, *ž*; *č*, *ǰ*. Sonorant consonants, on the other hand, are almost invariably voiced, although voiceless ones occur on occasion.

The voicing contrast in consonants is often accompanied by a difference in *tenseness*. This happens in most of the European languages where voiceless consonants are tense and voiced ones lax. Tense consonants are produced with greater muscular effort, and there may also be differences in the amount of subglottal pressure build-up. In other languages, the tenseness of consonants may be an independent parameter. Korean has voiceless stops which contrast in tenseness. The lax ones do have voiced variants, but only when they occur between vowels.

Secondary Vowel and Consonant Modifications

Many of the segments which we have described can be further modified by some secondary articulation superimposed onto the primary one.

One of the most common secondary vowel features is *nasalization*. In principle, any vowel can be nasalized. However, in those languages which have contrasts between oral and nasalized vowels, there are often more of the former. Not all the vowel heights may be represented in the nasalized system. In Standard French, for example, the nasalized vowels are all low: *un bon vin blanc* [œ̃ bɔ̃ vɛ̃ blã] 'a good white wine'. Nasalized vowels are also found in Portuguese, and in Yoruba and other languages of Africa. Phonetically nasalized vowels occur in English—for example, the vowel of *can*—where the nasalization is allophonic, due to the vowel's being contiguous to a nasal consonant. Allophonic secondary modifications are not infrequent. For example, *voiceless* vowels, which appear between voiceless consonants, occur in Japanese and Comanche.

Secondary articulations with the body of the tongue constitute an important type of consonant modification. Fairly common is *palatalization* where, in addition to the primary constriction, there is a secondary narrowing of the body of the tongue at the palatal region. Consequently, palatalized consonants have a characteristic *y* or *i* coloring. The Slavic languages are well-known for their palatalized consonants. Russian has p^y, b^y, t^y, d^y, k^y, g^y, f^y, v^y,

s^y, z^y, m^y, n^y, l^y, r^y, which contrast with the corresponding plain consonants. Another secondary consonantal modification is *labialization* (lip rounding). Such consonants have a characteristic w or u coloring. Twi has a full series of labialized consonants—p^w, b^w, t^w, d^w, k^w, g^w, f^w, s^w, m^w, n^w, η^w, h^w—which contrast with the corresponding plain ones. In Nupe, spoken in Nigeria, there are contrasts between plain, palatalized, and labialized consonants.

Secondary articulations resembling the laryngeal glides may constitute a type of consonant modification. An *aspirated* consonant gives the impression of being followed by h. In English, aspiration is always allophonic, but some languages utilize aspiration for phonemic distinctions. Thai has voiceless aspirated stops p^h, t^h, k^h, which contrast with voiceless unaspirated p, t, k, and with voiced b, d, g. Aspiration as a secondary modification usually affects only stops and affricates.

Glottalized consonants have a secondary closure at the glottis, in addition to the primary constriction higher up. The oral closure is released first, then the glottal closure, producing the double "popping" associated with these sounds. Many languages of Africa and of America have glottalized consonants, which are usually stops or affricates. Zuni has $p^{\prime}$, $t^{\prime}$, $k^{\prime}$, $k^{w\prime}$, $ts^{\prime}$, $c^{\prime}$, which contrast with the corresponding plain consonants.

Vowel-like and Consonant-like Properties

The dichotomy between vowel and consonant is one of the most fundamental divisions in describing types of sounds. Although these two classes differ in important ways, they also share much in common, since both types of segments are produced by the same articulatory mechanism. The similarities and differences between vowels and consonants can be identified by examining four properties: (1) sonority, (2) syllabicity, (3) degree of constriction, and (4) place of articulation. In comparing different consonants it will be convenient to refer to a property as more vowel-like or more consonant-like.

Sonority is a vowel-like quality, vowels being the most sonorous sounds. Among the consonants, *obstruents*—the stops, fricatives, affricates, and laryngeal glides—are less sonorous, more consonant-like, whereas *sonorants*—the nasals, liquids, and semivowels—are more resonant, more vowel-like. Sonorant sounds are almost always voiced.

Syllabicity is also a vowel-like quality, for, in general, vowels function as *syllabics* and consonants do not. However, the more vowel-like sonorant consonants—nasals and liquids—may on occasion function as syllabics. (A syllabic semivowel would be a high vowel.) The more consonant-like obstruents would rarely function as syllabics.

Constriction in the oral cavity is a consonant-like feature since consonants generally have closer articulation than vowels. The more consonant-like of the constrictions are total occlusion—the stops, affricates, nasals, and liquids—and frication—the fricatives and affricates. These *consonantal* constrictions in the oral cavity differentiate these consonants from the glides and the vowels, which have either less narrowing in the oral cavity—the semivowels and vowels—or no constriction in the oral cavity—the laryngeal glides.

Both vowels and consonants, except for laryngeal glides, are articulated at some place in the oral cavity. Vowel-like articulations are in the posterior part of the oral cavity, near the palatal and velar regions, where front and back vowels are made. Consonants with this vowel-like articulation are the palato-alveolars, palatals, velars, and uvulars. Consonant-like articulations are in the anterior part of the oral cavity. Anterior consonants are the labials, dentals, and alveolars. A vowel-like articulator is the body of the tongue or the lips. Consonants with this vowel-like articulator are the palatals, velars, uvulars, and labials. A consonant-like articulator is the blade of the tongue. *Coronal* consonants are the dentals, alveolars, and palato-alveolars.

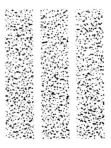

Distinctive Features

Is the Segment Indivisible?

One of our basic assumptions has been that an utterance is composed of a sequence of discrete segments. It might seem, then, that the segment is the smallest unit of phonological analysis, not further decomposable into anything smaller. This view suggests that segments ought to differ randomly from one another. Yet this is not the case. If we compare *p*, *t*, *k* with *p*, *r*, *š*, the members of the former set have an internal relationship which the members of the latter lack, for the former share the property of being voiceless stops.

You might argue that *p*, *t*, *k* fortuitously form a class only because of the particular phonetic traits we happened to pick for classifying sounds. But these phonetic categories are not so arbitrary, for if they are properly chosen they will have more than just a simple classificatory or cataloguing function. These same categories can account for different kinds of phonological processes observed in language. In English it is precisely *p*, *t*, *k* which, as phonemes, have aspirated allophones in certain contexts. Or *k* alternates with *s* in certain environments—*electric, electricity*. Under exactly the same conditions the other velar stop, *g*, is in alternation—*analogous, analogy*. Hence, *k* and *g* also form a class. We can now appreciate in what sense phonology has its foundations in phonetics.

Features as the Building Blocks
of Utterances

Once it becomes evident that it is advantageous to view segments as composed of sets of properties rather than as indivisible entities, we can show the relationships by listing explicitly the properties or *features* for each segment.

p	b	d	n
labial	labial	dental	dental
stop	stop	stop	nasal
voiceless	voiced	voiced	voiced

Then we can compare segments for similarities and differences. For example, *p* and *b* are both labial stops differing in voicing, *b* and *d* are both voiced stops differing in place of articulation, *d* and *n* are both voiced dentals differing in their manner of articulation, and *p* and *n* do not have anything in common.

Are the phonetic parameters set up in the preceding chapter sufficient as a set of features? By and large, yes, but some refinements are required. We sometimes described the same articulation with different terms: dentals were also referred to as anterior and coronal, or a syllabic semivowel turned out to be a vowel, or palatalized as applied to consonants had articulatory similarities to front as applied to vowels. So there is a bit of housekeeping to be done in order to determine which of the competing terms is most appropriate.

The appropriate features ideally fulfil three functions. (1) They are capable of describing the systematic phonetics—a phonetic function. (2) At the more abstract level they serve to differentiate lexical items—a phonemic function. (3) They define natural classes, that is, those segments which as a group undergo similar phonological processes. The difficulty is to find the set of features which, in the most insightful way, can fulfil all three of these requirements.

If we look at our phonetic parameters, we can extract two types of features: those which come in pairs and represent the presence or absence of an attribute, such as nasal-oral, voiced-voiceless, tense-lax, aspirated-unaspirated, rounded-unrounded, back-front, or sonorant-obstruent, and those which represent values along a scale, such as high, mid, low for vowels, or the place of articulation features for consonants—labial, dental, palato-alveolar, velar, and so on.

Binary Features

For features indicating opposite traits, we can employ a binary system (pluses and minuses) to show whether or not the attribute is present. Instead of two separate labels, such as voiced and voiceless, we need set up only a single feature, [voiced]; then voiced sounds can be specified as [+ voiced] and voiceless ones as [− voiced]. The binary notation is ideal for all features indicating opposite qualities. The advantage of a binary system is that one can show explicitly how members of pairs, such as voiced-voiceless or nasal-oral, are related to each other in a way in which other possible pairings, such as voiced-oral or voiceless-nasal, are not. Each natural pair, such as voiced-voiceless, is characterized by a single feature—in this case [voiced]—and the two members of the pair are differentiated by the value (+ or −).

The simplicity of the binary system allows us to inquire whether all features, including those which at first are not obviously binary, such as the height features for vowels or the place of articulation features for consonants, are capable of a binary interpretation. This question was first answered affirmatively by Jakobson. In presenting his original set of distinctive features, he made the strong claim that "the dichotomous scale is superimposed by language upon the sound matter." Chomsky and Halle also maintain that features are binary, but only at the classificatory or systematic phonemic level, whereas at the systematic phonetic level they need not be. In this chapter we will be concerned with the more common of the Chomsky–Halle "binary" features. Are these features the appropriate ones? We will try to point out some of the pros and cons.

The Major Class Features

SYLLABIC, SONORANT, CONSONANTAL

At the conclusion of the last chapter, we noted that similarities and differences between vowels and consonants can be indicated by reference to properties relating to syllabicity, sonority, and type of constriction. The three features, [syllabic], [sonorant], and [consonantal], encompass these properties. The feature [syllabic] characterizes the role a segment plays in the structure of the syllable. In general, vowels are [+ syllabic], whereas consonants are [− syllabic]. This feature is also necessary for differentiating syllabic nasals and liquids ([+ syllabic]) from their nonsyllabic counterparts. The feature [sonorant] refers to the resonant quality of a sound. Vowels are always [+ sonorant], as are nasals, liquids, and semivowels. The obstruents—stops, fricatives, affricates, and laryngeal glides—are, of course, [− sonorant]. The feature [consonantal] refers to a *narrowed constriction* in the *oral cavity*—either total occlusion or frication. Stops, fricatives, affricates, nasals, and liquids are [+ consonantal]. Vowels and semivowels, without this degree of narrowing, are [− consonantal]. Laryngeal glides are also classified as [− consonantal] as they have no constriction within the oral cavity.

	Oral cavity obstruents	Nasals, Liquids	Syllabic nasals, Liquids	Laryngeal glides	Semi-vowels	Vowels
Syllabic	−	−	+	−	−	+
Sonorant	−	+	+	−	+	+
Consonantal	+	+	+	−	−	−

A set of features makes explicit claims concerning the relationships of different segment types. The more feature values shared by different classes, the more they have in common. Thus, classes which differ in only one feature value are more closely related than those which differ in two or three feature values. Consider how the features, [syllabic], [sonorant], and [consonantal], relate the various major classes.

1. Obstruents and vowels are maximally opposed, because they have opposite values for each of the three features.
2. Laryngeal glides and semivowels are similar; they differ only in the value for [sonorant]. They thus constitute the class of glides.
3. Among the glides, semivowels are more closely related to vowels than are laryngeal glides. Semivowels and vowels differ only in the value for [syllabic], whereas laryngeal glides (as well as nasal and liquid consonants) differ from vowels in two features. Hence, semivowels are the most vowel-like of the consonants.
4. Among the glides, laryngeal glides are more closely related to obstruents than are semivowels. Laryngeal glides differ from obstruents in the value for [consonantal], whereas semivowels and obstruents differ in two feature values. This close relationship between laryngeal glides and obstruents is in accord with the observation that *ʔ* and *h* often function like true obstruents.
5. Nasal and liquid consonants are more like obstruents than syllabic nasals and liquids are. The former group is opposed to obstruents in the value for [sonorant], whereas the latter is opposed in two feature values.
6. Syllabic nasals and liquids are more like vowels than nasal and liquid consonants are. The former group is opposed to vowels in the value for [consonantal], whereas the latter is opposed in two feature values.
7. Semivowels are related to vowels in the same way that nasal and liquid consonants are related to syllabic nasals and liquids. The difference resides in the value for the feature [syllabic].

The features [syllabic] and [sonorant] appear well motivated. In those languages in which vowels are always syllabic and consonants nonsyllabic, the

specification [+ syllabic] becomes the formal means for referring to vowels and
[− syllabic] to consonants. In languages which have syllabic nasals and liquids,
they, along with vowels, may carry stress or tone. The feature [+ syllabic] then
refers to all these segments. In many languages sequences of obstruents must
have the same voicing. In German, all obstruents at the end of a word are
voiceless. The specification [− sonorant] captures this natural class. In
Russian consonants are palatalized before front vowels and *y*. The specification [− consonantal] comprises the class of vowels and semivowels and it is
common for these to function together. However, this specification also
includes the laryngeal glides (although there happen to be none in Russian).
It is not certain whether all three would ever behave similarly in languages with
vowels, semivowels, and laryngeal glides.

Manner Features

CONTINUANT, DELAYED RELEASE, STRIDENT, NASAL, LATERAL

The features [sonorant] and [consonantal] will distinguish obstruents from
sonorants, and glides from other consonants. Among obstruents we still need
to distinguish stops, fricatives, and affricates; for sonorant consonants which
are not semivowels we have to differentiate nasals from liquids, and, for the
latter, laterals from nonlaterals.

   Among the obstruents are those with continuous frication throughout
([+ continuant])—the fricatives—and those beginning with total occlusion
([− continuant])—the stops and affricates. This feature also distinguishes ʔ
[− continuant] from *h* [+ continuant]. Although stops and affricates both
begin with total occlusion, they are released differently. Affricates have a
delayed release ([+ delayed release]); stops are released instantaneously
([− delayed release]). Further distinctions have to be made among the continuants. In particular, we must distinguish bilabial φ from labiodental *f*,
dental θ from alveolar *s*, palatal ç from palato-alveolar *š*, and velar *x* from
uvular *X*. In Chapter 2 (p. 18) we noted that the first member of each pair
is nonstrident, whereas the second member is strident, due to the outgoing air
hitting the teeth or the uvula. For affricates the delayed fricative release is
almost always strident. In those few languages with contrasts involving
strident and nonstrident affricates, the feature [strident] also serves to differentiate these two types. The features [consonantal], [continuant], [delayed
release], and [strident], then, define different types of obstruents. (Blanks in
the matrix mean that the particular feature plays no role in classifying the
segment.)

	t	t^θ	t^s	θ	s	$\textsf{ʔ}$	h
Sonorant	−	−	−	−	−	−	−
Consonantal	+	+	+	+	+	−	−
Continuant	−	−	−	+	+	−	+
Delayed release	−	+	+				
Strident		−	+	−	+		

The features [nasal] and [lateral] differentiate various of the sonorant consonants. Nasals are opposed to liquids as [+ nasal] to [− nasal]. (This feature also differentiates nasalized vowels [+ nasal] from oral ones [− nasal].) Among liquids, laterals are opposed to nonlaterals as [+ lateral] to [− lateral]. The features [consonantal], [nasal], and [lateral] define the different types of sonorant consonants.

	y	n	l	r
Sonorant	+	+	+	+
Consonantal	−	+	+	+
Nasal		+	−	−
Lateral			+	−

The features [continuant], [nasal], and [lateral] are reasonably straight-forward in what they do. More novel are [delayed release] and [strident]. The specification [− continuant] conveniently forms a natural class of stops and affricates, as opposed to the fricatives. In English, for example, *č* is aspirated in the same environment as *p*, *t*, *k*. But since the release of an affricate resembles a fricative, there is good reason to want to include affricates and fricatives in a natural class. This feature system does not allow this unless these segments are specified as [+ strident]. This ploy would not work for any language having both strident and nonstrident fricatives and affricates.

Place of Articulation Features

ANTERIOR, CORONAL

Chomsky and Halle classify the four principal places for consonant articula-tion—labial, dental, palato-alveolar, and velar—according to whether the constriction is at the extreme forward region of the oral cavity (the *anterior* consonants) or more retracted (the *nonanteriors*), and furthermore, whether the articulator is the blade of the tongue (the *coronals*) or some other articulator (the *noncoronals*).

	p	t	č	k
Anterior	+	+	−	−
Coronal	−	+	+	−

Dentals and velars are maximally opposed, as are labials and palato-alveolars. All other pairs have a feature specification in common. Although labials and palato-alveolars do not seem to constitute a natural class, it is not so certain that dentals and velars should be excluded in this way. For example, it is not uncommon for both to become palatalized before front vowels—note rege*nt*, rege*n*cy; electri*c*, electri*c*ity. The relationship between labials and other consonants is also not evident. Labials and dentals (the [+ anterior] consonants in this system) do not function particularly as a natural class. Furthermore, the feature [anterior] is not well motivated phonetically. The "forward part of the oral cavity" is a rather vague and arbitrary designation. On the other hand, there is some evidence for grouping together labials and velars (the [− coronal] consonants). For example, in consonant clusters Latin *k* passed to *p* in Rumanian—Latin *laktem*, Rumanian *lapte* 'milk'. Another weakness is in the characterization of labials. Within this sytem there is no way to show the relationship among labials, labialized consonants, and rounded vowels and semivowels.

Body of Tongue Features

HIGH, LOW, BACK, AND LIP SHAPE FEATURE: ROUND

In the classification of vowels, we made use of the parameters high, mid, low, front, back, rounded, and unrounded. The parameters relating to backness and rounding are of course binary.

	i	ü	u	ɨ
Back	−	−	+	+
Round	−	+	+	−

Since, at most, two degrees (a + value and a − value) can be distinguished for a given single feature, in order to differentiate three degrees, such as high, mid, and low, we need to use two features conjointly, specifying values for both. If we take the two extreme degrees of vowel height, *high* and *low*, and set these up as independent features, we can interpret within a binary framework the original three parameters.

	High Vowels	Mid Vowels	Low Vowels
High	+	−	−
Low	−	−	+

In a binary system utilizing two features, one ought to be able to distinguish a maximum of four entities. But the fourth possibility, a vowel which is [+ high] and [+ low], is excluded. The articulation underlying this configuration is impossible, since the tongue cannot simultaneously be raised and lowered. That is, whereas a segment could be neither high nor low (i.e., mid), no segment could be both high and low.

If there are languages with four vowel heights, this feature system cannot accommodate them. Ladefoged has argued that vowel height may be a ternary (or quaternary [?]) feature, and that setting up [high] and [low] as separate features becomes a maneuver for forcing a multivalued feature into a binary straitjacket.

Semivowels are similar to high vowels, except for syllabicity. Consequently, the features [high], [back], and [round] will also differentiate the various semivowels.

	i	y	ü	ẅ	u	w
Syllabic	+	−	+	−	+	−
Consonantal	−	−	−	−	−	−
High	+	+	+	+	+	+
Back	−	−	−	−	+	+
Round	−	−	+	+	+	+

The body of the tongue and the lips are involved in the secondary consonant modifications of palatalization and labialization, the superposition of a *y*-like or *w*-like coloring onto the primary articulation. The features [high], [back], and [round] further characterize these secondary modifications.

	p	pʸ	pʷ	t	tʸ	tʷ	k	kʸ	kʷ
Anterior	+	+	+	+	+	+	−	−	−
Coronal	−	−	−	+	+	+	−	−	−
High	−	+	+	−	+	+	+	+	+
Back	−	−	+	−	−	+	+	−	+
Round	−	−	+	−	−	+	−	−	+

Finally, the body of the tongue is an articulator for [− anterior, − coronal] consonants—palatals, velars, and uvulars. For palatals the body of the tongue is raised ([+ high]) at the palatal region ([− back]), for velars it is raised ($[+$ high]) at the velar region ($[+$ back]), whereas for uvulars it is not raised ($[-$ high]) but is still retracted ($[+$ back]).

	Palatal	Velar	Uvular
Anterior	−	−	−
Coronal	−	−	−
High	+	+	−
Back	−	+	+

Chomsky and Halle note that when labials and dentals are palatalized they retain their original place of articulation and acquire a secondary palatalization. On the other hand, when velars are palatalized they undergo a shift in place of articulation and become palatals. These changes are nicely captured in this feature system. Notice that the specification given above for k^y is the same as that given for palatals.

Subsidiary Features

Tense, Voiced, Aspirated, Glottalized

$[+$ tense] = tense $[-$ tense] = lax
$[+$ voiced] = voiced $[-$ voiced] = voiceless
$[+$ aspirated] = aspirated $[-$ aspirated] = unaspirated
$[+$ glottalized] = glottalized $[-$ glottalized] = nonglottalized

The feature [tense] occurs with both vowels and consonants. This feature can also be used for the nonlateral liquids, to distinguish a trilled *r* ($[+$ tense]) from a flap ($[-$ tense]). The feature [voiced] occurs with all types of segments, although it is more rare for sonorants to have voicing differences. The features [aspirated] and [glottalized], which go by different names in *Sound Pattern of English*, are uniquely used with consonants, and most of the time only with obstruents. It would be advantageous if these two features could somehow be explicitly related to *h* and *?*, respectively. Chomsky and Halle list a few other features with which we will not be concerned here, and they also propose features for dealing with exoticisms such as the African clicks.

Prosodic Features

For prosodic features we need to recognize [stress] and [long]. Stressed vowels will be marked $[+$ stress] and long segments will, of course, be $[+$ long]. As we shall not be dealing with tone languages we will not postulate any tone features, some of which have been proposed by Wang and by Fromkin.

Why Distinctive Features?

To find the appropriate set of features is indeed a task. There is nothing sacred about the particular set we have presented. Others, such as the Jakobsonian binary distinctive features, have been proposed in the past, and we can no doubt expect future revisions. Yet we hope that we have not left the impression that a set of features is arrived at through the whim of the linguist. It may be worthwhile to emphasize again the various criteria brought to bear in choosing features.

1. The features have their foundation in phonetics. A feature may have articulatory (e.g., [coronal], [high]), acoustic (e.g., [sonorant], [strident]), or perceptual (e.g., [syllabic], [stress]) correlates.
2. The features must be adequate for characterizing important phonetic differences between languages. The Italian *r* is phonetically a dental trill, whereas in Standard French the *r* is a uvular trill. A feature system must distinguish these two different trills even if they never occur together in the same language.
3. The features must accommodate the principal allophones of a language. In English, a feature [aspirated] is needed even though it never functions contrastively.
4. Since features serve to categorize the contrasting segments (phonemes) of a language, the set of features must accommodate all the necessary contrasts within the system. This requirement is probably met if conditions 2 and 3 are satisfied. It is condition 4 which has led to all features being binary, since a binary system allows one to state simply whether a segment has membership in a particular category. Feature systems which are not binary have been proposed. The traditional classificatory schema, in which there are three vowel heights or various places of articulation for consonants, is a nonbinary classification.
5. Segments which share phonetic traits often undergo the same phonological processes. A set of features must provide the appropriate *natural classes* for stating these phonological changes. In English, the plural ending has three different manifestations: (1) *ɨz* after *s, z, š, ž, č, ǰ* (e.g., class*es*, ros*es*, ash*es*, garag*es*, church*es*, judg*es*); (2) *s* after voiceless sounds other than those in (1) (e.g., cap*s*, cat*s*, cake*s*, cuff*s*, fourth*s*), and (3) *z* after voiced sounds other than those in (1) (e.g., robe*s*, road*s*, rogue*s*, slave*s*, path*s*, dame*s*, cane*s*, ring*s*,

bear*s*, bell*s*, cow*s*, dye*s*, sofa*s*). The six segments after which *iz* is added can be characterized as a natural class within our feature system. These six are the only segments in English which are [+ coronal, + strident]. By the same token, *s* is added after segments which are [− voiced], and *z* after segments which are [+ voiced]. Allophonic variants of phonemes frequently fall into natural classes. In English, *p*, *t*, *k*, and *č*, are phonetically aspirated in certain environments. As a class, these segments share the feature specifications [− continuant, − voiced].

As a natural class becomes more inclusive, fewer features are needed to characterize it. Thus, *i* is specified as [+ syllabic, − consonantal, + high, − low, − back, − round]; the class containing *i* and *e* as [+ syllabic, − consonantal, − low, − back, − round]; the class comprising *i*, *e*, and *æ* as [+ syllabic, − consonantal, − back, − round]; the class including *i, e, æ, ü, ö*, and *œ* as [+ syllabic, − consonantal, − back], the class of all vowels as [+ syllabic, − consonantal]; and the class of all segments which can function as syllable peaks as [+ syllabic].

The Simplicity Metric

The relationship between a class and the number of features needed to specify it suggests a simplicity metric for formally characterizing the "naturalness" of a class. As a class becomes more general, more inclusive, the notation for the class also becomes more general, with fewer formal symbols needed to specify it. The idea that the complexity of the notation should directly reflect the degree of linguistic "generalization" has become an important theoretical issue within generative phonology, an issue we shall take up in subsequent chapters.

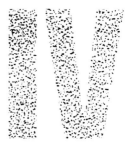

Redundancy

Distinctive Feature Matrices

We can formally represent a phonological system as a matrix, in which the columns stand for phonemes and the rows for distinctive features. A + or − entry in a particular cell (where a column and a row intersect) indicates whether that phoneme possesses the property or feature in question. Consider a language with a five-vowel system, such as Spanish. The matrix indicates only those features which serve to differentiate the various vowels.

	i	e	a	o	u
High	+	−	−	−	+
Low	−	−	+	−	−
Back	−	−	+	+	+
Round	−	−	−	+	+

No two segments may have identical specifications for all the features; otherwise, they would not be distinguished. Minimally, two different segments must be opposed in the value for at least one feature. Thus, *i* and *e* have identical specifications for all features except [high]. Of course, segments could differ in several or even all feature specifications; for example, *i* and *a* differ in values for three features.

Segment Redundancy

The preceding matrix is fully specified—every segment has a value stated for each feature. However, all of these specifications are not independent. Some of the values can be predicted on the basis of values for other features. Consequently, the matrix contains a certain amount of *redundancy*. We repeat the basic five-vowel system, circling the redundant values.

	i	e	a	o	u
High	+	−	⊖	−	+
Low	⊖	⊖	+	⊖	⊖
Back	−	−	⊕	⊕	⊕
Round	⊖	⊖	⊖	+	+

In this matrix the following dependencies hold: (a) a segment which is [+ high] is always [− low]; (b) a segment which is [+ low] is always [− high]; (c) a segment which is [− back] is always [− round]; (d) a segment which is [+ round] is always [+ back]; (e) since there is only one low vowel, a segment which is [+ low] is also [+ back] and [− round]; (f) as there are no front low vowels, a segment which is [− back] is always [− low]; and (g) because there are no rounded low vowels, a segment which is [+ round] is always [− low]. Observe that the set of nonredundant (noncircled) features exhibits an interesting symmetry.

We can develop a notation for formally expressing these redundancies. The downward arrow is to be read as "is also" or "implies."

(a)   [+ high]
   ↓
  [− low]

(b)   [+ low]
   ↓
  [− high]

(c)   [− back]
   ↓
  [− round]

(d)   [+ round]
   ↓
  [+ back]

(e)   [+ low]
  ↓
 $\begin{bmatrix} + \text{ back} \\ - \text{ round} \end{bmatrix}$

(f, g) $\begin{Bmatrix} [- \text{ back }] \\ [+ \text{ round}] \end{Bmatrix}$
   ↓
  [− low]

Just as the nonredundant specification of the matrix exhibits symmetry, so does the formalized statement of redundancies. Pairs of statements are "inversely" symmetrical. For (a)(b) and for (c)(d) the features are switched and take on opposite values in relation to the arrow. This inverse symmetry follows logically from the fact that if *A* is not *B*, then *B* is not *A* (or if high is not low, then low is not high). In the case of the final pair, a conjunction of features under the arrow in (e) becomes a disjunction above the arrow in (f, g), $\begin{bmatrix} + \text{ back} \\ - \text{ round} \end{bmatrix}$ entails *both* back *and* nonround, whereas $\left\{ \begin{matrix} [- \text{ back}] \\ [+ \text{ round}] \end{matrix} \right\}$ is to be read *either* nonback *or* round.

Although the circled features in the matrix are redundant, this does not mean that we are not interested in their values, or that these values are not significant, but only that they are predictable from other values. Redundant features may be important whenever we need to make reference to a natural class comprising several segments. For example, if we want to refer to the class containing all vowels except *a*, we would specify this class as those segments which are [− low], even though in the matrix these values are redundant. Similarly, we would refer to *i, e, a* as the [− round] vowels. On the other hand, a convenient way to refer to one particular segment is to specify the non-redundant values. For example, it suffices to characterize *i* as [+ high, − back], provided, of course, we are dealing with a five-vowel system. Features which are redundant in the five-vowel system need not be so for some other vowel pattern.

Language-Specific and Universal
Redundancies

We can distinguish between redundancies which are *language-specific* or system-specific and those which are *universal*. Language-specific redundancies exist because all theoretically possible combinations of features are not always utilized.

Hungarian has four stop phonemes.

	p	t	c	k
Anterior	+	+	−	−
Coronal	−	+	+	−

The features [anterior] and [coronal] are maximally utilized—two features with two values differentiate four entities. English, unlike Hungarian, has no palato-alveolar stop (although it does have a palato-alveolar affricate). In English, the features [anterior] and [coronal] will not be maximally used *for the stops*, so the English matrix will contain redundancies not found in the Hungarian.

	p	t	k
Anterior	+	⊕	−
Coronal	−	+	⊖

Since velars are the only stops in English which are [− anterior], it follows that if a stop is [− anterior] it is also [− coronal]. Similarly, because dentals are the only stops which are [+ coronal], a stop which is [+ coronal] must also be [+ anterior].

Universal redundancies express co-occurrence restrictions on combinations of features. Consider the features [high] and [low], which conjointly specify the three vowel heights. The fact that vowels which are specified [+ high] are always [− low] and vowels which are specified [+ low] are always [− high] is due to the articulatory constraint that the body of the tongue cannot be simultaneously raised and lowered. Another universal redundancy is that vowels (the segments which are [+ syllabic, − consonantal]) are always [+ sonorant].

Not all features are *relevant* for characterizing all classes of sounds. For example, the features [continuant], [delayed release], and [strident] do not differentiate vowels, so values for these three features *need never be specified* for vowels. Consequently, a specification such as [+ continuant] or [− strident] suffices to indicate that we are dealing with a consonant.

Distinctiveness versus Distinguishability

The notion of segment redundancy has had an interesting history within generative phonology. We shall trace this development by considering a fairly simple example, the height specifications for the three front unrounded vowels.

	i	e	æ
High	+	−	−
Low	−	−	+

Within this system we can extract two redundancies: [+ high] is [− low], and [+ low] is [− high].

In the early days of generative phonology, when Halle first discussed segment redundancies, he proposed as part of the "simplicity metric" (see p. 34) that redundant feature specifications, since they are predicted by rule, should not appear originally in the matrix, but should instead be left blank. The blanks would subsequently be filled in with the appropriate plus or minus values in accordance with the segment redundancy statements.

	i	e	æ
High	+	−	
Low		−	+

Halle imposed as a further constraint that these matrices conform to a "distinctiveness" condition: In the partially specified (redundant-free) matrix each pair of segments must be opposed in the value for at least one feature.

Our partially specified matrix violates this condition. Although *i* and *e* are distinct (differing in values for [high]) and *e* and æ are distinct (differing in values for [low]), *i* and æ are *not* distinct, for each is uniquely specified for a feature for which the other is blank.

Once distinctiveness becomes a condition imposed on partially specified matrices, then the only permitted matrices would be one of the following:

	i	e	æ		ı	e	æ
High	+	−	−		+	−	
Low		−	+		−	−	+

Comparing these to the previous matrix, we find at least two things wrong here. It is arbitrary which of the two distinct matrices is selected, but, more important, not all redundancy has been fully extracted.

Why should the distinctiveness condition have been imposed? Because it was thought that if segments were not pair-wise distinct, the blanks could be improperly used. For example, what would prevent us from setting up the following partially specified matrix?

	i	e	æ
High	+	−	
Low			+

The three blanks can be filled in by the segment redundancies:

[+ high]	[− high]	[+ low]
↓	↓	↓
[− low]	[− low]	[− high]

The culprit here is the second redundancy statement, which permits referring uniquely to *e* with the specification [− high]. This means that through this one feature *e* is opposed to both *i* and æ: *e* as [− high] is opposed to *i* as [+ high] and to æ as blank [high]. In actuality, the blank here is functioning as a third (improper) value.

The misuse of blanks is an issue separate from that of determining the minimal specification for *distinguishing* segments. If we adopt the point of view that redundancy statements must make valid generalizations *even for completely specified matrices*, then, of the three segment redundancy statements given, [+ high] is [− low] and [+ low] is [− high] hold true for the fully specified matrix, whereas [− high] is [− low] does not, for æ is [− high] without also being [− low]. Once we accept that segment redundancy statements must hold true for a fully specified matrix, blanks can no longer be improperly used. The whole problem of "distinctiveness" versus "distinguishability" was first raised by Stanley, who convincingly demonstrated that the only appropriate constraint on redundant-free matrices is one based on distinguishability.

Sequence Redundancy

Redundancies *within a segment* are not the only ones to be extracted. There are also redundancies *across segments*, due to restrictions on permitted sequences of phonemes. For example, there is no English word which begins with ten consonants, nor is there one which begins with even four consonants. The limit is three, as exemplified by words such as *spl*it, *str*ing, *scr*am. Furthermore, the consonants which can appear in these initial clusters are highly constrained: the first one can only be *s*, the second must be *p*, *t*, or *k*, and the third is restricted to *r* or *l*.

Part of "knowing" English is knowing the permitted sequence of segments. Neither *strib* nor *ftrib* is an actual word of English. Yet the former qualifies as a potential word, while the latter does not, for it violates the constraint that words beginning with three consonants have *s* as the initial one. We could imagine a new soap called *Strib*, but it is unlikely that any advertising agency would latch onto *Ftrib* as a name for its product.

Segment redundancies and *sequence redundancies* together constitute the morpheme structure conditions of a language. Before turning to these conditions we need to digress for a moment to talk about the morpheme.

Morphemes

Morphology considers how words are built from smaller constituents. The component parts of words are *morphemes* (e.g., bases, stems, prefixes, suffixes, plural endings, past tense endings). The word *phone* is composed of one morpheme, *phon+ic* of two, *phon+et+ic* of three, *phon+et+ic+s* of four *allo+phone* of two, and so on. *Jump* contains a single morpheme, but the past form *jump+ed* is composed of two morphemes.

Frequently, one of the component morphemes in words containing several morphemes also occurs in isolation as an independent word. However, this need not be the situation. The following words are all composed of a prefix plus the stem *-ceive*.

> re+ceive
> de+ceive
> con+ceive
> per+ceive

The prefixes *re-*, *de-*, *con-*, and *per-* are not confined to *-ceive*, but occur as well in other forms.

remit			permit
refer	defer	confer	
retain	detain	contain	pertain

(Incidentally, we can deduce that *-mit*, *-fer*, and *-tain* are also stems.)

The Lexicon

The *lexicon* of a language is a list of its morphemes. For each morpheme information is given about its meaning, syntactic properties, morphological properties, exceptional behavior (if any), and pronunciation. For the moment we shall be concerned only with the last type of information.

The phonological representation of a morpheme can be viewed as a two-dimensional matrix in which the columns stand for the segments of the morpheme, and the rows list the features. A specification within a square of the matrix indicates whether the segment possesses the feature in question. A blank means that the feature is not relevant for that segment. The phonological matrix for the morpheme *strip* might look something like this:

	s	*t*	*r*	*i*	*p*
Syllabic	−	−	−	+	−
Consonantal	+	+	+	−	+
Sonorant	−	−	+	+	−
Continuant	+	−			−
Delayed release		−			−

	s	*t*	*r*	*i*	*p*
Strident	+				
Nasal			−	−	
Lateral			−		
Anterior	+	+	−		+
Coronal	+	+	+		−
High	−	−	−	+	−
Low	−	−	−	−	−
Back	−	−	−	−	−
Round	−	−	−	−	−
Tense	+	+	−	−	+
Voiced	−	−	+	+	−

We will continue to use unit symbols, such as *s* and *i*, to represent segments in isolation, as well as sequences of unit symbols to represent morphemes. However, it should be kept in mind that the unit symbols are to be interpreted as bundles of specified features.

Sequence Redundancy Conditions

Having considered the morpheme and its role in the lexicon, we are now ready to return to the original problem: stating constraints on sequences of segments. We will take up two types of constraints, *syllable structure conditions* and *if-then conditions*.

The restriction on the number of initial consonants is an example of a syllable structure constraint. English morphemes may begin with zero, one, two, or three consonants—*it*, *pit*, *spit*, *split*—but there are no morphemes beginning with four or more consonants—**splrit*. (An asterisk indicates an impossible form.) The following formula states this aspect of English syllable structure.

(a) + ([− syllabic]) ([− syllabic]) ([− syllabic]) [+ syllabic]

Parenthesized elements may or may not be present. The + at the beginning of the formula represents the morpheme boundary and indicates that the segment which follows the boundary is initial.

It is, of course, not sufficient to state that morphemes may have up to three initial consonants. If there are clusters, we need to be more specific and to indicate precisely the restrictions on the types of consonants which can appear in each position. It is the *if-then* conditions which narrow down these sequential constraints. These state that *if* a particular condition obtains in a certain environment, *then* some other condition must also be met. For example, *if* a morpheme begins with three consonants, *then* the first one must be *s*, the second a voiceless stop, and the third a liquid.

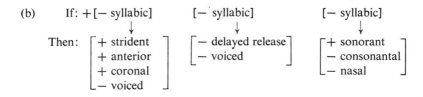

In the *then* part of the rule, we have not mentioned all the features for characterizing the particular segments, but have used only the minimum specification. Any additional features are predicted from the segment redundancies. For example, for the first segment, it is enough to identify *s* as [+ strident, + anterior, + coronal, − voiced], i.e., as a voiceless dental strident. We know that any segment possessing these features must also be [− syllablic, − sonorant, + consonantal, + continuant, etc.]. For the second segment, one need only specify voiceless stops as [−delayed release, − voiced]. Any segment which is [− delayed release] must also be [− syllabic, − sonorant, + consonantal, − continuant].

There appear to be clusters in which the third consonant is a semivowel— *skew* [skyūw], *squat* [skwãt]. However, these segments have a highly restricted distribution. In such clusters, the *y* is always followed by *ū*, and the *w* is always preceded by *k*. Because of these restrictions, it is possible to analyze [yūw] as a triphthong and [kw] as a labialized velar, an analysis which precludes treating the [y] or [w] of these clusters as independent consonants.

Conceivable Morphemes

The segment redundancies and the sequence redundancies jointly form a set of *morpheme structure conditions.* The former define the set of possible phonemes in a language and the latter the set of possible morphemes—that is, possible sequences of phonemes. A *conceivable morpheme* can now be defined as an arbitrary sequence of bundles of specified features which does not violate any of the morpheme structure conditions of that language. In English, *küb* is not a conceivable morpheme. The vowel would be specified as [+ high, − low, − back, + round]. The + value for [round] violates a segment redundancy stating that [− back] vowels are always [− round]. Nor could *splrit* qualify as a possible morpheme. It violates sequence redundancy (a), since the fourth segment is not specified as [+ syllabic]. The sequence *ftrib* could not be a morpheme of English, either. Although it does not violate the constraint of beginning with at most three consonants, it does violate sequence redundancy (b); the first obstruent is not *s*. Finally, although *strib* is not an actual word of English, it qualifies as a conceivable English word. There is no morpheme structure condition with which *strib* is in conflict.

Partially versus Fully Specified
Lexical Matrices

At one time, it was believed that the lexical matrices for morphemes should be partially specified—that is, redundant values should not be shown. What made this idea attractive was that one could see immediately for any morpheme which features of a segment were predictable and which were not. The unspecified values would then be supplied from the morpheme structure conditions. Since it is preferable not to mark in the lexicon what can be predicted, it appeared to make sense to leave predictable values unspecified. Having partially specified lexical matrices also suggested a natural *evaluation metric* for lexical representations: The most highly valued lexicon would be the one having the greatest number of unspecified features with the least number of morpheme structure conditions.

Stanley has shown that there are difficulties with partially specified lexical matrices. Inconsistencies may arise due to the interaction of segment redundancies with sequence redundancies. In English, *s* has to be specified as [+ strident] to distinguish it from θ, which is [− strident). Because *s* is strident, we can predict that it is [− syllabic]. Therefore, if there were partially specified lexical matrices, it would appear that *s* should be entered as [+ strident], with the value for the feature [syllabic] unspecified. However, there is a sequence redundancy stipulating that if there are three [− syllabic] segments in morpheme initial position, then the first one must be *s* [+ strident, + anterior, + coronal, − voiced]. Hence, in these clusters, the feature [strident] could be left unspecified. A contradiction now arises in that *s* cannot be simultaneously unspecified for the feature [syllabic]—as required by the segment redundancy—and for the feature [strident]—as required by the sequence redundancy. The value for one or the other would have to be indicated in clusters, but which one?

To resolve such difficulties, all lexical representations, except for irrelevant features, are to be fully specified. One cannot then count unspecified features as a way of evaluating the optimal lexical representation. Instead, the most highly valued lexicon is the one in which the least number of morpheme structure conditions characterizes the greatest number of lexical entries.

Why Redundancy?

The more features operating to distinguish segments, the more different those segments are and the greater their perceptual distance. Because language must be used under all kinds of nonideal conditions—conversations in a noisy room, whispering behind someone's back, trying to talk and eat at once—the more the redundancy, the easier becomes the task of discriminating between segments. In fact, a redundant feature may play a more important role in perception than a nonredundant one. The aspiration of initial stops is redundant in English, being conditioned by voicelessness. Yet, perceptually, the aspiration is probably the main clue for identifying these initial segments.

But redundancy in language is not something simply imposed onto the code in order to make it efficient and practical. A good deal of sequence redundancy, for example, is a consequence of internal constraints on the physical functioning of the vocal mechanism. That languages rarely have words beginning with more than three consonants can be attributed to the inability of humans to produce long sequences of consonants without intervening vowels. Even where consonant sequences occur, some types are inherently easier to produce than others. Many languages have initial clusters of a stop followed by a liquid, but an initial sequence of a liquid followed by a stop would be rare if not impossible. Its impossibility, or at least rarity, doubtless has a physiological explanation. In addition to these "inherent" constraints, each language will have its own particular redundancies. It is primarily these language-specific redundancies, both sequential and segmental, that are captured through the morpheme structure conditions.

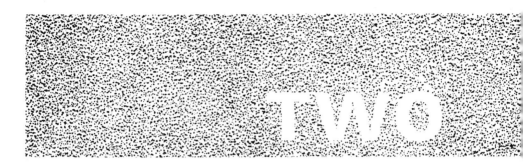

Dynamic Phonology

Phonological Processes

When morphemes are combined to form words, the segments of neighboring morphemes become juxtaposed and sometimes undergo change. Consider the morphologically related forms *electric, electrical, electricity*, and *fanatic, fanatical, fanaticism.* Here the final *k* of *electric* and *fanatic* becomes *s* before a morpheme beginning with *i*. Changes also occur in environments other than those in which two morphemes come together—for example, word initial and word final positions, or the relation of a segment vis-à-vis a stressed vowel. All such changes will be called *phonological processes.*

In an effort to avoid a bewildering array of disparate types, we will organize phonological processes into four categories: *assimilation*, where segments become more alike; *syllable structure*, where there is alteration in the distribution of consonants and vowels; *weakening and strengthening*, where segments are modified according to their position in the word; and *neutralization*, where segments merge in a particular environment. Examples of these processes are drawn from synchronic descriptions as well as from historical change.

Assimilation

In *assimilatory processes* a segment takes on features from a neighboring segment. A consonant may pick up features from a vowel, a vowel may take on features of a consonant, one consonant may influence another, or one vowel may have an effect on another.

CONSONANT ASSIMILATES VOWEL FEATURES

Features of a vowel may be extended onto a consonant as secondary modifications. Palatalization and labialization are common processes of this type. In palatalization, the tongue position of a front vowel is superimposed on an adjacent consonant; in labialization, the lip position of a rounded vowel induces a secondary articulation onto the consonant.

In Russian, certain consonants become palatalized whenever they precede a front vowel.

stó*l*	table (*nominative singular*)	sto*l*ʸé	table (*locative singular*)
vkú*s*	taste (*noun*)	vkú*s*ʸen	tasty
dá*r*	gift	da*r*ʸít	to give
dó*m*	house	do*m*ʸísko	cottage
bó*m*ba	bomb	bom*b*ʸít	to bomb

In Nupe, a West African language, consonants are palatalized before front vowels and labialized before rounded ones.

eg^y i	child	eg^w u	mud
eg^y e	beer	eg^w o	grass
	ega	stranger	

In English, the alternations exemplified in electri*c*, electri*c*ity, and analo*g*ous, analo*g*y reflect a historical palatalization followed by a shift in place of articulation.

VOWEL ASSIMILATES CONSONANT FEATURES

Features from a consonant may be superimposed on a vowel. In this kind of assimilation, the modification of the vowel is usually allophonic.

It is quite common for vowels to be phonetically nasalized when adjacent to a nasal consonant, a process which occurs in English: *see* [sīy], *seen* [sĩyn]; *cat* [kæt], *can't* [kæ̃nt].

In Chatino, spoken in Mexico, unstressed vowels are voiceless between voiceless consonants.

t*i*yé*?*	lime	t*i*hí	hard
k*i*nó	sandal	k*i̥*sú	avocado
s*u*wí	clean	s*u̥*ʔwá	you send
la*?*á	side	tḁ*?*á	fiesta
ŋg*u*tá	seed	k*u̥*tá	you will give
k*i*ʔ	fire	k*i̥*tá	you will wait

CONSONANT ASSIMILATES CONSONANT FEATURES

One of the most widespread phenomena is for consonant clusters to agree in voicing. This process can be seen in English where the endings for the plural, third person singular, and past tense agree in voicing with a preceding consonant. Thus, one finds *s* and *t* after voiceless consonants, *z* and *d* after voiced ones.

kʌp*s*	cups	kʌb*z*	cubs
pæt*s*	pats	pæd*z*	pads
bæk*t*	backed	bæg*d*	bagged
rēys*t*	raced	rēyz*d*	raised

It is common for a nasal consonant to become homorganic with a following consonant—that is, the nasal adopts the same place of articulation. Yoruba, spoken in West Africa, has a nasal prefix which assimilates in this fashion.

ba	hide	*m*ba	is hiding
fɔ	break	*m*fɔ	is breaking
tɛ	spread	*n*tɛ	is spreading
sun	sleep	*n*sun	is sleeping
lɔ	go	*n*lɔ	is going
kɔ	write	*ŋ*kɔ	is writing
gun	climb	*ŋ*gun	is climbing
wa	come	*ŋ*wa	is coming

In English, the negative prefix *in-* becomes homorganic to a following stop: e.g., *inadvisable*, but *impossible, imbalance, intolerance, indecisive, incoherent*, the last with *ŋ* for some speakers.

VOWEL ASSIMILATES VOWEL FEATURES

The vowel of one syllable may become more like the vowel of some other syllable. Here we can distinguish *vowel harmony* from *umlauting*.

Vowel harmony is a case in which vowels agree in certain features. In Turkish, the high vowels of a suffix agree in backness and rounding with the stem vowel.

diš	tooth	d*i*š*i*m	my tooth
ev	house	*e*v*i*m	my house
gönül	heart	gön*ü*l*ü*m	my heart
göz	eye	göz*ü*m	my eye
baš	head	ba*š*i*m	my head
gul	rose	g*u*l*u*m	my rose
kol	arm	kol*u*m	my arm

In German, back vowels are fronted before certain suffixes containing a high front vowel; this is known as *umlaı*

y*ā*r	year	yǣrliç	annual
št*u*ndə	hour	št*ü*ndliç	hourly
g*ū*t	good	g*ǖ*tik	kind
n*ō*t	need	n*ȫ*tik	necessary
g*o*t	god	götin	goddess
h*u*nt	dog	hündin	bitch

In modern German, umlauting is no longer restricted to a following high front vowel, although it is believed that all the umlauting environments did arise in this way.

In English, irregular plurals such as *foot, feet* and *mouse, mice* are vestiges of an umlauting process which was fairly extensive in Old English.

Syllable Structure Processes

Syllable structure processes affect the relative distribution of consonants and vowels within the word. Consonants or vowels may be deleted or inserted. Two segments may coalesce into a single segment. A segment may change major class features, such as a vowel becoming a glide. Two segments may interchange. Any of these processes could cause an alteration in the original syllable structure.

We shall consider CV syllable structure—a syllable containing a single consonant and vowel—to be basic. Any process which takes a more complex syllabic structure and reduces it to the CV pattern leads to a *preferred syllable structure*. The effect of such processes is to break up clusters of consonants or sequences of vowels. For example, a cluster of two consonants could be simplified in one of three ways: one of the consonants could be deleted, a vowel could be inserted between the two consonants, or the two consonants could coalesce into a single segment.

CONSONANT DELETION

Words in French may terminate in a consonant. For many words this final consonant is dropped if the following word begins with a consonant. The result is CV syllable structure between words.

pǝti*r* ami	little friend	pǝti garsɔ̃	little boy
gro*z* ami	big friend	gro garsɔ̃	big boy
tro*p* etrwa	too narrow	tro laržǝ	too wide
trɛ*z* etrwa	very narrow	trɛ laržǝ	very wide

The word final consonant is also dropped at the end of a phrase (i.e., before a pause) or when the word is spoken in isolation; consequently, words frequently end in open syllables.

il ɛ pǝti	he is little
il ɛ gro	he is big
sɛ tro	it's too much
trɛ	very

In some *r*-less dialects of English, word final *r* is dropped before a consonant or in phrase final position, but not before a vowel: e.g., *father came, I saw father, father arrived.* The distribution of the indefinite article also conforms to preferred syllable structure: *an* apple, *a* banana.

VOWEL DELETION

In French, the vowel of the definite article, *le* or *la*, is deleted whenever the following word begins with a vowel, thus preventing two vowels from coming together.

lǝ garsɔ̃	the boy	l ami	the friend (*masculine*)
la fiyǝ	the girl	l ami	the friend (*feminine*)

Certain English morphemes terminating in a vowel drop the vowel before a suffix beginning with a vowel: *Mexico, Mexican* (derived from *Mexico+an*); *cello, cellist* (*cello+ist*).

Consonant Insertion (epenthesis)

In Hanunoo, spoken in the Philippines, the consonant *h* is inserted to break up a vowel cluster. Note what happens when the suffix *i* is added in the last two forms.

ʔupat	four	ʔupati	make it four
ʔunum	six	ʔunumi	make it six
ʔusa	one	ʔusa*h*i	make it one
tulu	three	tulu*h*i	make it three

Alternatively, one might maintain that the suffix is -*hi* and that the *h* is dropped after stems terminating in a consonant.

In some dialects of English, *r* is inserted whenever a word ending in a schwa is followed by a word beginning with a vowel: e.g., *the idea came, the idea-r-is good.*

Vowel Insertion (epenthesis)

Latin words cannot end in a consonant-liquid cluster. In such cases, the vowel *e* is inserted to break up this cluster. Note the nominative forms where there is no overt ending for the nominative case.

patris	father (*genitive*)	pater	father (*nominative*)
agrī	field (*genitive*)	ager	field (*nominative*)
librī	book (*genitive*)	liber	book (*nominative*)

In English, schwa is inserted between final consonant-sonorant clusters: e.g., *central, center* [sentər]; *cyclic, cycle* [sāykəl]; *spasmic, spasm* [spæzəm]. That the schwa is inserted, rather than deleted, in a medial syllable can be seen by comparing *wintry* with *watery*; the latter exhibits schwa in the medial syllable as well.

Consonant Coalescence

Two contiguous consonants are replaced by a single one which shares features of the two original ones. Hence, coalescence involves a kind of assimilation. In Korean, whenever a noncontinuant and *h* are contiguous they are replaced by an aspirated noncontinuant.

na*k*	fall	+ *h*wa	flower	→ na*k*ʰwa	fallen flower
ku*p*	bend	+ *h*ita	(*causative suffix*)	→ ku*p*ʰita	to bend
čo*h*	good	+ *k*o	and	→ čo*k*ʰo	good and
no*h*	to lay	+ *t*a	(*verb ending*)	→ no*t*ʰa	to lay (eggs)

Other frequent examples of consonant coalescence include: a consonant plus glottal stop coalescing to a glottalized consonant; a consonant plus *y* to a palatalized consonant; a consonant plus *w* to a labialized consonant; and a stop plus fricative to an affricate.

In English, morpheme final *t*, *d*, *s*, and *z* and a following *y* are replaced by palato-alveolar fricatives. This is particularly evident before the suffix-*ion*: e.g., *relate, relation* [rəlēyšən]; *evade, evasion* [əvēyžən]; *regress, regression* [rəgrešən]; *confuse, confusion* [kənfyūwžən].

Two identical consonants often coalesce to a single one. In the development of French, the Latin geminates were *degeminated*.

Latin	French	
te*rr*a	tɛrə	land
be*ll*a	bɛlə	beautiful (*feminine*)
gu*tt*a	gutə	drop
pre*ss*a	prɛsə	press

For the English prefix *in*-, the *n* assimilates to a following liquid: e.g., *irresponsible, illegal*. In the spoken language these geminate clusters have become degeminated.

Vowel Coalescence

Latin *ai* and *au* became *e* and *o* respectively in Romance. The resulting vowel has the same backness and rounding as the original high vowel. Because the vowel clusters have been reduced to a single vowel, the new syllabic structure is simpler.

Latin	Spanish	
*ai*difíkium	*e*difísio	building
*ai*kʷálem	*e*guál	even
k*áu*sa	k*ó*sa	thing
p*áu*pere	p*ó*bre	poor

Coalescence of Vowel and Consonant

In French, a vowel plus nasal consonant is replaced by a nasalized vowel. This process occurs whenever the nasal consonant is followed by a consonant or a pause. Here is another way by which French arrives at its preferred syllabic structure. (In French, nasalized vowels are always low.)

bɔnœr	happiness	bɔ̃te	goodness
tɔnalite	tonality	tɔ̃	tone
rɔmanistə	Romanist	rɔmã	Romance (*masculine*)
plɛnə	full (*feminine*)	plɛ̃	full (*masculine*)
finə	fine (*feminine*)	fɛ̃	fine (*masculine*)

Since coalescence involves both assimilation and reduction, many of these examples could be described as the joint action of these two processes. Consider the change in which a vowel plus nasal consonant becomes a nasalized vowel. First there is assimilation—the vowel becomes nasalized before the nasal consonant—and the nasal consonant is then deleted. Historically, the nasalized vowels of French did evolve in this way. However, there is not sufficient evidence to suggest that all types of coalescence should be treated as assimilation followed by deletion.

MAJOR CLASS CHANGES

A segment may change major class membership. It is quite common for high vowels and lateral liquids to become glides. In French, unstressed high vowels are converted to the corresponding semivowels if they are followed by a vowel. Through this process certain vowel sequences are avoided.

sí	saws	syé	to saw
žú	plays	žwé	to play
tü	kills	twé	to kill

In English, unstressed prevocalic *i* becomes *y* after *l*, but not after *r*: e.g., *criterion, clarion; pavilion* [pəvĭlyən]; *battalion* [bətælyən].

A sonorant consonant may become syllabic when adjacent to a nonsyllabic. This change has been claimed for Proto-Indo-European (Seivers' Law). Analogously, one might want to consider the final syllables of such English words as *center, cycle,* and *spasm* as terminating in consonant and syllabic sonorant—[sĕntr̩], [sāykl̩], [spæzm̩]—rather than consonant-schwa-consonant.

METATHESIS

Two segments may interchange. In Hanunoo (see also p. 54), a sequence of glottal stop plus consonant becomes consonant plus glottal stop. This metathesis is likely to be the prelude to a subsequent coalescence whereby the consonant plus glottal stop becomes a glottalized consonant, a unit segment, thereby simplifying the syllable structure.

ʔusa	one	kas ʔa	once
ʔupat	four	kap ʔat	four times
ʔunum	six	kan ʔum	six times
tulu	three	katlu	three times

In the preceding forms the stems for the numerals are *ʔsa, ʔpat, ʔnum, tlu*. Because consonant clusters are not permitted in word initial position, an epenthetic *u* is inserted to break up the nonpermissible cluster (column 1). The morpheme meaning "times" is *ka*, which precedes the morpheme for the numeral (column 2). Consonant clusters may occur here since they are not in word initial position. However, the sequence glottal stop plus consonant metathesizes (e.g., *ka* + *ʔsa → kas ʔa*), but other consonant sequences do not (e.g., *ka + tlu*).

Weakening and Strengthening

Not all changes in syllabic structure necessarily lead to a simpler syllable structure. The syllable structure would become more complex, for example, if a vowel in an original CVCV configuration were to be deleted so that two consonants came together. Such deletions are often caused by segments occupying a weak position in the syllable. In the following processes the important factor is the weakening, and any changes in syllable structure are incidental.

SYNCOPE AND APOCOPE

In syncope a vowel near a stressed vowel is deleted. This phenomenon occurred in the development from Latin to French. In words with antepenultimate stress—where the stress is on the third syllable from the end of the word—the penultimate vowel, or the vowel between the stressed and final vowels, was dropped.

Latin	French	
pópulum	pœ́plə	people
tábula	táblə	table
pérdere	pérdrə	to lose
árborem	árbrə	tree

In English, when the stressed syllable is followed by two unstressed ones, the vowel immediately following the stressed syllable is often dropped in colloquial speech, particularly if it is followed by a single sonorant consonant: e.g., *chocolate, choc'late; happening, happ'ning; every, ev'ry; nursery, nurs'ry*.

Apocope is the loss of a final unstressed vowel, most often a reduced or schwa-like vowel. In colloquial French final schwa is usually dropped, whereas it would not necessarily be in more formal styles.

Formal French	Colloquial French	
eglizə	egliz	church
ružə	ruž	red
tablə	tabl	table
fiyə	fiy	girl

VOWEL REDUCTION

Vowel reduction involves the weakening of unstressed vowels to schwa. English displays morphological alternations between a stressed full vowel and an unstressed reduced (schwa) vowel.

éybəl	able	əbílətīy	ability
kǽnədə	Canada	kənéydīyən	Canadian
fówtəgræf	photograph	fətágrəfīy	photography
súwpər	super	səpíyrīyər	superior
sówbər	sober	səbráyitīy	sobriety
dəkɔ́rəm	decorum	dékərəs	decorous

DIPHTHONGIZATION

Stressed vowels and tense vowels are the strong ones. Whereas weak vowels may undergo syncope, apocope, or reduction, strong vowels frequently diphthongize.

In Romance, Latin *e* and *o* became diphthongs in certain environments. Italian diphthongization took place when the vowel was *stressed* and in an open syllable: *e* became *ye* and *o* became *wo*. The glide which developed has the same backness and rounding as the following vowel.

Latin	Italian	
wénet	vyéne	comes
mélem	myéle	honey
bóna	bwóna	good (*feminine*)
nówa	nwóva	new (*feminine*)

In English, the tense vowels *i, e, u,* and *o* phonetically are often diphthongs: [īy], [ēy], [ūw], [ōw]. Here too the glides have the same backness and rounding as the vowel.

VOWEL SHIFT

Stressed vowels may change position in the vowel space. In late Middle English, stressed tense vowels underwent the Great Vowel Shift. These vowels took a clockwise turn in the height dimension: low vowels became mid, mid vowels became high, and high vowels became low (ultimately the diphthongs *āy* and *āw*). The resulting low diphthongs have been centralized.

The effects of the Great Vowel Shift are easily observed in words of French or Latin origin.

Romance form	English	
divín	dəváyn	divine
serén	səríyn	serene
profǽn	prəféyn	profane
profúnd	prəfáwnd	profound
provɔ́k	prəvówk	provoke

The stressed lax (short) vowels of Classical Latin shifted downward in Vulgar Latin: high vowels become mid, mid vowels became low, and low vowels remained low. The tense (long) vowels did not undergo vowel shift. Distinctions in vowel length were lost in Vulgar Latin, and consequently some of the vowels merged.

Classical Latin $\bar{\imath}$ $\breve{\imath}$ $\bar{e}$ $\breve{e}$ $\bar{a}$ $\breve{a}$ $\breve{o}$ $\bar{o}$ $\breve{u}$ $\bar{u}$

Vulgar Latin i e ε a $ɔ$ o u

Neutralization

Neutralization is a process whereby phonological distinctions are reduced in a particular environment. Hence, segments which contrast in one environment have the same representation in the environment of neutralization.

CONSONANT NEUTRALIZATION

Neutralization of word final obstruents takes place in German. In initial and intervocalic positions, voiced and voiceless obstruents are in contrast. Only voiceless ones are found in word final position, so in this environment there is neutralization between pairs of voiced and voiceless obstruents.

bun*t*ə	colorful (*attributive*)	bun*t*	colorful (*predicative*)
bun*d*ə	league (*dative*)	bun*t*	league (*nominative*)
tā*g*ə	days	tā*k*	day
štar*k*ə	strong (*attributive*)	štar*k*	strong (*predicative*)
lum*p*ən	rascals	lum*p*	rascal
šter*b*ən	to die	štar*p*	died
grō*s*ə	big (*attributive*)	grō*s*	big (*predicative*)
glǣ*z*ər	glasses	glā*s*	glass

VOWEL NEUTRALIZATION

Russian has a five-vowel system for its stressed vowels. When these vowels appear in unstressed position there is neutralization: Both *i* and *e* appear as *i*, both *a* and *o* appear as *a*, and *u* remains *u*. Thus, in unstressed position, Russian goes from a five-vowel to a three-vowel system. (Russian also neutralizes voicing of obstruents in word final position.)

sn^y*é*k	snow	sn^y*i*gá	snows
l^y*é*s	forest	l^y*i*sá	forests
gl*á*s	eye	gl*a*zá	eyes
g*ó*rat	town	g*a*radá	towns
*ó*straf	island	*a*stravá	islands
l*ú*k	onion	l*u*ká	onions

In French, all nasalized vowels are low. Different oral vowels may have the same nasalized partner. Hence, there is neutralization in tongue height for the nasalized vowels.

f*i*nɛs	fineness	fɛ̃	fine (masculine)
pl*e*nitüd	fullness	plɛ̃	full (masculine)
sərɛnə	serene (*feminine*)	sərɛ̃	serene (*masculine*)
romanistə	Romanist	romã	Romance (*masculine*)
brünir	to turn brown	brɑ̃	brown (*masculine*)
žönə	fast (*noun*)	zɑ̃	fasting

There appears to be an interrelationship between neutralization and assimilation, or between neutralization and weak position. Where obstruent clusters agree in voicing, contrasts in voicing are neutralized. By the same token, if a nasal consonant becomes homorganic to a following consonant, then nasal consonants of different places of articulation can no longer contrast in those environments, and one could view this assimilation as a type of neutralization. In Russian, vowel neutralization affects the unstressed vowels, which are weaker than stressed ones. In English, unstressed vowels reduce. This process is also neutralization, since different unstressed vowels all merge to schwa. Nasalized vowels are perceptually more obscure, hence weaker, than oral vowels. Nasalized vowels are neutralized in French. It may be that all neutralizations could be subsumed under either assimilation or weakening.

We have by no means surveyed all the processes reported for languages. For example, we have not treated *dissimilation*, in which segments become less similar to each other. We have merely tried to give a sampling of some of the common processes recurring in diverse languages.

Why Languages Undergo
Phonological Processes

Most phonological processes can be explained as articulatory or perceptual phenomena. Assimilation has a natural explanation in coarticulation. During the formation of a sound, the articulatory organs may be anticipating the articulation for another sound, and consequently the first sound will be modified in the direction of the second, or the articulation of the first may be carried over into that of the second. Coarticulation effects are readily observed when consonants become palatalized or labialized before palatal (front) or labial (rounded) vowels, or vowels are nasalized in the vicinity of a nasal consonant, or the place of articulation for a consonant induces a similar place of articulation on a preceding nasal. Other kinds of assimilation may be related to inherent constraints on the articulatory mechanism. In languages which have voicing contrasts for obstruents, invariably in clusters, the distinctions are neutralized and all obstruents must agree in voicing. This type of assimilation appears to be a consequence of inherent difficulties in adjusting the glottis for different voicing states for sequences of segments of the same type.

Other phonological processes can be explained through perception. Segments which are maximally differentiated, which are perceptually more opposed to one another, are more stable than those which are less differentiated. Stressed vowels are perceptually stronger than unstressed ones. The former frequently diphthongize, a process which makes them even more perceptible. Unstressed vowels have less perceptual distance among themselves, and may therefore be neutralized, a process leading to fewer vowels, but with greater perceptual distance between adjacent ones. Or unstressed vowels may reduce to schwa, thus being maximally opposed to tense vowels, as in French, or they may drop out altogether. There are also interrelations between articulation and perception. The optimal articulatory contrast is that between a closed vocal tract and an opened one, in other words, between consonants and vowels. Processes for preferred syllable structure lead to this optimal alternation.

Phonological Rules

If we can state the exact conditions under which a phonological process takes place, we have in effect given a rule. So far, the changes have been stated in ordinary language; we now convert these statements into a formal notation. The notation must be suitable for expressing the kinds of processes which take place in phonology, and for capturing the generalizations found there. We shall consider four types of rules: feature changing rules, rules for deletion and insertion, rules for permutation and coalescence, and rules with variables. Because so many rules will involve reference to the major divisions of consonants and vowels, as a notational convention we will use C and V for consonant and vowel.

Feature Changing Rules

When segments undergo change, we want to know three things: (1) which segments change; (2) how they change; and (3) under what conditions they change. The segment or class of segments which undergoes change is characterized by the minimal set of features necessary for unique identification. The change is also expressed in feature notation. What changes and how it changes are then connected by an arrow pointing in the direction of the change.

The following two rules state that obstruents become voiceless and that vowels become nasalized.

$$[- \text{ sonorant}] \rightarrow [- \text{ voiced}]$$
$$V \rightarrow [+ \text{ nasal}]$$

These rules imply that all obstruents become voiceless in all positions and that all vowels become nasalized wherever they occur. Most processes, however, are not so unrestricted, and the change takes place only in certain contexts. A diagonal slash is used to separate the environment from the rest of the rule. If the change takes place adjacent to some other segments, then those segments constitute the environment. In French, one of the environments for vowel nasalization is one in which the vowel precedes a nasal consonant which is in turn followed by a consonant. (In the environment part of the rule the place where the change occurs is indicated by a dash.)

$$V \rightarrow [+\ \text{nasal}]/\ \underline{\hspace{1cm}}\ \begin{bmatrix} C \\ +\ \text{nasal} \end{bmatrix} C$$

The following rule states that obstruents are voiced in intervocalic position.

$$[-\ \text{sonorant}] \rightarrow [+\ \text{voiced}]/V\ \underline{\hspace{1cm}}\ V$$

In umlauting, vowels become fronted by a following *i*.

$$V \rightarrow [-\ \text{back}]/\ \underline{\hspace{1cm}}\ C_0 \begin{bmatrix} V \\ +\ \text{high} \\ -\ \text{back} \end{bmatrix}$$

In this rule the subscript zero on the C means that zero or more consonants may be found between the vowel which is umlauted and the vowel of the environment. Thus, $\underline{\hspace{1cm}}\ C_0 \begin{bmatrix} V \\ +\ \text{high} \\ -\ \text{back} \end{bmatrix}$ is an abbreviation for an infinite number of environments.

$$\underline{\hspace{1cm}}\ \begin{bmatrix} V \\ +\ \text{high} \\ -\ \text{back} \end{bmatrix}$$

$$\underline{\hspace{1cm}}\ C \begin{bmatrix} V \\ +\ \text{high} \\ -\ \text{back} \end{bmatrix}$$

$$\underline{\hspace{1cm}}\ CC \begin{bmatrix} V \\ +\ \text{high} \\ -\ \text{back} \end{bmatrix}$$

$$\underline{\hspace{1cm}}\ CCC \begin{bmatrix} V \\ +\ \text{high} \\ -\ \text{back} \end{bmatrix}, \text{etc.}$$

C_0 invariably appears in rules in which we wish to make a statement about the vowels of adjacent syllables, but are not interested in the consonantal structure of the syllable. What is relevant in this particular rule is that a vowel is influenced by the vowel in the following syllable. The actual number of consonants (and there could be none) which occurs between the two vowels is not relevant. Although C_0 allows an infinite number of consonants, no language would ever have more than a few consonants separating the vowels. C_0 should be interpreted, then, as a notational device for expressing the notion "irrespective of the number of consonants."

Segments are not the only elements which occur in the environment. We often need to know whether the process takes place in word initial or word final position, at the pause, or at a morpheme boundary. Therefore, we will have to have symbols for boundaries. We use + for morpheme boundary, $\#$ for word boundary, and $\|$ for phrase boundary or pause.

In French, a vowel is also nasalized if the following nasal consonant ends the word.

$$V \rightarrow [+ \text{ nasal}]/ \underline{\quad} \begin{bmatrix} C \\ + \text{ nasal} \end{bmatrix} \#$$

THE BRACE NOTATION

We have written two vowel nasalization rules for French.

$$V \rightarrow [+ \text{ nasal}]/ \underline{\quad} \begin{bmatrix} C \\ + \text{ nasal} \end{bmatrix} C$$

$$V \rightarrow [+ \text{ nasal}]/ \underline{\quad} \begin{bmatrix} C \\ + \text{ nasal} \end{bmatrix} \#$$

These two rules are similar in that they both state that the vowel must be followed by a nasal consonant and in turn by something else. Rather than having two separate statements for vowel nasalization, we should prefer a single statement showing what is common to both nasalization processes, as well as the way in which they differ. In other words, we would like to say that in French a vowel becomes nasalized if it is followed by a nasal consonant and either a consonant or a word boundary. Braces are the device used in rules for referring to alternate environments. The following rule now captures the relevant aspects of vowel nasalization in French.

$$V \rightarrow [+ \text{ nasal}]/ \underline{\quad} \begin{bmatrix} C \\ + \text{ nasal} \end{bmatrix} \begin{Bmatrix} C \\ \# \end{Bmatrix}$$

THE PARENTHESIS NOTATION

Words in French are stressed on one of the last two syllables. For words terminating in schwa the stress is on the vowel preceding the schwa. Otherwise, the stress is on the vowel of the final syllable. (In French, schwa is the only lax vowel.)

$$V \rightarrow [+ \text{ stress}]/ \underline{\hspace{1cm}} C_0 \begin{bmatrix} V \\ - \text{ tense} \end{bmatrix} \#$$

$$V \rightarrow [+ \text{ stress}] \underline{\hspace{1cm}} C_0 \#$$

The two rules involve the same process—the assignment of stress. They differ only in that the first rule mentions a lax vowel whereas the second rule lacks this specification. By having two separate rules we are missing this generalization. Parentheses are used as a formal device for collapsing two similar rules when one contains a specification lacking in the other. This notation will allow us to make a single statement for stress assignment in French.

$$V \rightarrow [+ \text{ stress}]/ \underline{\hspace{1cm}} C_0 \left(\begin{bmatrix} V \\ - \text{ tense} \end{bmatrix} \right) \#$$

Braces and parentheses are formal means for collapsing rules which are partly similar and partly different. Where braces are used, each rule to be collapsed contains restrictions not found in the other. With parentheses, only one of the rules has an additional restriction. These notations are employed only for collapsing rules involving the same process, and not any two rules accidentally sharing common features. Thus, with braces we collapsed rules involving nasalization, and with parentheses rules assigning stress. It would be incorrect to try to collapse nasalization and stress into one rule, even though each of these processes mentions V to the left of the arrow, as these are separate, unrelated phenomena. In Chapter 8 we shall see that these abbreviatory notations also make claims about rule ordering.

Rules for Deletion
and Insertion

Deletion is indicated by $\emptyset$, the null symbol. The segment which undergoes deletion appears to the left of the arrow, and the $\emptyset$ to the right.

In French, nasal consonants are deleted after nasalized vowels.

$$\begin{bmatrix} C \\ + \text{ nasal} \end{bmatrix} \rightarrow \emptyset / \begin{bmatrix} V \\ + \text{ nasal} \end{bmatrix} \underline{\hspace{1cm}}$$

Also in French, certain word final consonants are deleted before a following consonant or in phrase final position.

$$C \rightarrow \emptyset \underline{\quad} \# \begin{Bmatrix} C \\ \| \end{Bmatrix}$$

In a rule for insertion, the null symbol appears to the left of the arrow and the segment to be inserted appears to the right. In Hanunoo, when two consonants begin the word, the vowel *u* is inserted to break up the consonant cluster.

$$\emptyset \rightarrow \begin{bmatrix} V \\ + \text{ high} \\ + \text{ round} \end{bmatrix} / \# C \underline{\quad} C$$

Rules for Permutation and Coalescence

TRANSFORMATIONAL RULES

The rule $A \rightarrow B/ \underline{\quad} C$ is equivalent to $AC \rightarrow BC$, where the environment is mentioned on both sides of the arrow. The rule which nasalizes a vowel when it precedes a nasal consonant and a word boundary is given in this alternate notation.

$$V \begin{bmatrix} C \\ + \text{ nasal} \end{bmatrix} \# \rightarrow \begin{bmatrix} V \\ + \text{ nasal} \end{bmatrix} \begin{bmatrix} C \\ + \text{ nasal} \end{bmatrix} \#$$

Of course, there is a lot of repetition in stating the rule this way. The nasal consonant and the word boundary need to be indicated on both sides of the arrow. That the vowel has become nasalized is new information, but the fact that it still needs to be specified as a vowel on the right repeats what is known on the left. If we were to adopt this format for writing rules, we would want to find a notation in which identical information does not have to be repeated on both sides. Essentially, we would like to say that if there are three entities in a row, and the first is a vowel, the second a nasal consonant, and the third a word boundary, then the first segment becomes nasalized, but the second and third elements remain intact and unchanged. We can do this by *specifying* and *numbering* the elements which appear to the left and using the *same* numbers on the right to refer to their relative positions. If one of the segments on the left undergoes a change, that change is indicated on the right along with that segment's number. For elements which do not change, just the number of the element appears on the right.

We rewrite the rule of French nasalization.

$$V\begin{bmatrix} C \\ + \text{nasal} \end{bmatrix} \# \rightarrow \begin{bmatrix} 1 \\ + \text{nasal} \end{bmatrix} 2 \quad 3$$
$$1 \qquad\qquad 2 \qquad 3$$

This notation can also be used for expressing deletion and insertion. For deletion, a ∅ appears in the right half of the rule in place of the segment which is to undergo deletion. We cite the French rule which deletes a word final consonant.

$$C \# \begin{cases} C \\ \| \end{cases} \rightarrow \emptyset \quad 2 \quad 3$$
$$1 \quad 2 \quad 3$$

In rules for insertion, no ∅ symbol is needed. A specification of the segment to be inserted is indicated in the right half of the rule at the correct place in the sequence. The rule in Hanunoo which inserts *u* between two consonants in word initial position can be given in this format.

$$\# \quad C \quad C \rightarrow 1 \quad 2 \begin{bmatrix} V \\ + \text{high} \\ + \text{round} \end{bmatrix} 3$$
$$1 \quad 2 \quad 3$$

The notation just developed is often referred to as the *transformational format*. It is similar to that used in syntax for writing transformational rules, and, in fact, the same operations are involved: insertion, deletion, partial change, and, as we shall see in a moment, permutation and coalescence. Where only *one* segment is undergoing change, the statement of the change in the transformational format is equivalent to the standard notation used earlier. We introduce the transformational format because it is needed for two types of processes which cannot be handled by the standard notation, namely, metathesis and coalescence, processes in which *two or more* segments are *simultaneously* affected.

METATHESIS AND COALESCENCE

In Hanunoo, the cluster glottal stop and consonant becomes consonant and glottal stop when it is internal to the word—that is, between vowels. The transformational format is ideal for expressing interchanges of this type.

$$V\begin{bmatrix} - \text{consonantal} \\ - \text{continuant} \end{bmatrix} CV \rightarrow 1 \quad 3 \quad 2 \quad 4$$
$$1 \qquad\qquad 2 \qquad 3\,4$$

Rules for coalescence, where two segments become one, also need to be stated in the transformational format. We shall view coalescence as a process in which one of the segments, the primary one, is modified, while the secondary segment is deleted. The modifications are indicated in the right half of the rule.

The following rule states that a consonant followed by *w* coalesces to a labialized consonant.

$$C \begin{bmatrix} - \text{ syllabic} \\ - \text{ consonantal} \\ + \text{ round} \end{bmatrix} \rightarrow \begin{bmatrix} 1 \\ + \text{ round} \end{bmatrix} \emptyset$$
$$\quad\ 1 \qquad\qquad 2$$

If vowel nasalization in French is viewed as coalescence rather than as assimilation and subsequent deletion, we can write a coalescence rule stating that a vowel and a following nasal consonant becomes a nasalized vowel when followed by another consonant or a word boundary.

$$V \begin{bmatrix} C \\ + \text{ nasal} \end{bmatrix} \begin{Bmatrix} C \\ \# \end{Bmatrix} \rightarrow \begin{bmatrix} 1 \\ + \text{ nasal} \end{bmatrix} \emptyset \quad 3$$
$$\quad\ 1 \qquad\ 2 \qquad 3$$

Rules with Variables

ASSIMILATION

Most obstruent clusters in French involve only two consonants. Where they differ in voicing the first consonant assimilates its voicing to the second; e.g., *bt → pt, gs → ks, ds → ts, kb → gb, tz → dz, bš → pš*. To express these assimilations we would need to write two separate rules—one stating assimilation before a voiced obstruent, the other before a voiceless one.

$$[- \text{ sonorant}] \rightarrow [+ \text{ voiced}] / \underline{\quad\quad} \begin{bmatrix} - \text{ sonorant} \\ + \text{ voiced} \end{bmatrix}$$

$$[- \text{ sonorant}] \rightarrow [- \text{ voiced}] / \underline{\quad\quad} \begin{bmatrix} - \text{ sonorant} \\ - \text{ voiced} \end{bmatrix}$$

Two separate rules miss the generalization that the first obstruent always has the *same* voicing as the second. We should like to state this by a single rule. We can see that the two separate rules are similar. They differ only in the value assigned to the feature [voiced] (wherever it has a + value in one rule, it has a − value in the other rule), but *not* in the features themselves. It is the complete

symmetry in the two rules on which we wish to base the generalization. Therefore, we shall adopt the following notation: If two rules are identical except
for the values of the same feature, then the two rules can be replaced by a single
rule. The values which are different in the two rules are replaced by a variable—
the Greek letter alpha—in the new rule.

$$[-\text{ sonorant}] \rightarrow [\alpha \text{ voiced}]/ \underline{\hspace{1cm}} \begin{bmatrix} -\text{ sonorant} \\ \alpha \text{ voiced} \end{bmatrix}$$

The variable α is the formal means for expressing the notion "has the same
value as" or "agrees in value with." Thus, the preceding rule says that the first
obstruent takes on the same value for the feature [voiced] as is found in the
second obstruent.

The variable notation may also be used in rules for deletion, insertion,
and coalescence. In Korean, there are diphthongs: *ye, ya, yo, yu; wi, we, wa.*
However, there are no diphthongs **yi* and **wu.* Whenever these would arise,
they become the corresponding simple vowels *i* and *u.* The glide is deleted if it
is followed by a high vowel of the same backness and rounding as the glide.

$$\begin{bmatrix} -\text{ syllabic} \\ -\text{ consonantal} \\ \alpha \text{ back} \\ \alpha \text{ round} \end{bmatrix} \rightarrow \emptyset / \underline{\hspace{1cm}} \begin{bmatrix} \text{V} \\ +\text{ high} \\ \alpha \text{ back} \\ \alpha \text{ round} \end{bmatrix}$$

The sequence **wo* does not occur in Korean either, so the rule would have to
be extended to handle this case as well.

In Italian, the stressed vowels ε and $\mathupsilon$ diphthongize in certain environments which need not concern us here: ε becomes *yε* and $\mathupsilon$ becomes *w$\mathupsilon$*. The
glide which develops agrees in backness and rounding with the following vowel.

$$\emptyset \rightarrow \begin{bmatrix} -\text{ syllabic} \\ -\text{ consonantal} \\ \alpha \text{ back} \\ \alpha \text{ round} \end{bmatrix} / \underline{\hspace{1cm}} \begin{bmatrix} \text{V} \\ +\text{ low} \\ \alpha \text{ back} \\ \alpha \text{ round} \end{bmatrix}$$

DISSIMILATION

Dissimilation is a process in which two segments become less similar to each
other. Consider a language which does not permit clusters of obstruents with
the same manner of articulation, so that stop-stop or fricative-fricative do not
occur. The second stop of a stop-stop cluster is replaced by the corresponding
fricative, and the second fricative of a fricative-fricative cluster is replaced by
the corresponding stop—e.g., *kp* → *kf, tt* → *ts, fs* → *ft, ss* → *st.* In obstruent
clusters, then, the second obstruent must have the opposite value for the feature
[continuant] from that found in the first obstruent. This dissimilation is

handled by the specification — α, which is the formal means for expressing the notion "oppposite in value to."

$$[- \text{sonorant}] \rightarrow [- \alpha \text{ continuant}]/[\alpha \text{ continuant}] \underline{\quad}$$

RULES WITH MULTIPLE VARIABLES

In some cases a segment may assimilate different values from two or more features of some segment. Consider the common rule in which a nasal consonant becomes homorganic to the following obstruent, taking on the obstruent's values for the features [anterior] and [coronal]. If the obstruent is a labial ([+ anterior, — coronal]), then the nasal must also have the value + for the feature [anterior] and — for the feature [coronal]; if the obstruent is a dental ([+ anterior, + coronal]), then the nasal must have the corresponding values. This also holds true for the palato-alveolars and velars. More than one variable is needed to express assimilations of this type. One uses as many variables as the number of features which can freely vary.

$$\begin{bmatrix} \text{C} \\ + \text{nasal} \end{bmatrix} \rightarrow \begin{bmatrix} \alpha \text{ anterior} \\ \beta \text{ coronal} \end{bmatrix} / \underline{\quad} \begin{bmatrix} - \text{sonorant} \\ \alpha \text{ anterior} \\ \beta \text{ coronal} \end{bmatrix}$$

The following rule, which makes use of a single variable on the features [anterior] and [coronal], says something quite different.

$$\begin{bmatrix} \text{C} \\ + \text{nasal} \end{bmatrix} \rightarrow \begin{bmatrix} \alpha \text{ anterior} \\ \alpha \text{ coronal} \end{bmatrix} / \underline{\quad} \begin{bmatrix} - \text{sonorant} \\ \alpha \text{ anterior} \\ \alpha \text{ coronal} \end{bmatrix}$$

This rule states that whenever the obstruent has *identical* values for the features [anterior] and [coronal], the nasal must also have the *same identical values*— that is, if the obstruent is [+ anterior, + coronal] or [— anterior, — coronal], the assimilation will take place. However, the assimilation would not occur if the obstruent has opposite values for the features [anterior] and [coronal]— that is, when the obstruent is [+ anterior, — coronal] or [— anterior, + coronal]. This rule would convert *mt* and *mk* to *nt* and *ŋk*, respectively, but would have no effect on *mp* or *mč*.

Vowel harmony in Turkish is another example of a rule requiring more than one variable. A high suffix vowel agrees in backness and rounding with the preceding vowel, so that if that vowel is [— back, — round], the suffix vowel is [— back, — round]; if that vowel is [— back, + round], the suffix vowel is [— back, + round], and so on

$$\begin{bmatrix} \text{V} \\ + \text{high} \end{bmatrix} \rightarrow \begin{bmatrix} \alpha \text{ back} \\ \beta \text{ round} \end{bmatrix} / \begin{bmatrix} \text{V} \\ \alpha \text{ back} \\ \beta \text{ round} \end{bmatrix} C_0 + C_0 \underline{\quad}$$

Two variables are required in Turkish, since in this language the features [back] and [round] work independently. Turkish has four classes of vowels: front unrounded, front rounded, back rounded, and back unrounded. In those languages which do not have mixed vowels and where all vowels except *a* are either front unrounded or back rounded, values for the features [back] and [round] for those vowels must always be the same—[α back, α round]. The examples presented previously, in which the glides *y* and *w* agreed in backness and rounding with vowels, were of this type.

EXCHANGE RULES

The variable notation is used for special kinds of rules known as *exchange rules*, *switching rules*, or *flip-flop rules*. These rules all have the form: $[\alpha X] \rightarrow [-\alpha X]$. In such rules, anything which is originally $[+ X]$ becomes $[- X]$ while, *simultaneously*, anything which starts out as $[- X]$ becomes $[+ X]$.

In English, there was the Great Vowel Shift (see p. 58) which affected stressed tense vowels that were front unrounded or back rounded. The low vowels æ and ɔ eventually became the mid vowels ē and ō, the original mid vowels became the high vowels ī and ū, and the two original high vowels become the low vowels æ and ɔ (actually, the diphthongs āy and āw). In order to simplify the discussion, we will only consider the changes in vowel height and ignore here the diphthongization of vowels as well as the centralizing of the resulting low diphthongs.

$$\begin{pmatrix} \bar{\imath} \\ \bar{e} \\ \bar{æ} \end{pmatrix} \qquad \bar{a} \qquad \begin{pmatrix} \bar{u} \\ \bar{o} \\ \bar{ɔ} \end{pmatrix}$$

Chomsky and Halle describe this shift through two exchange rules. First, the high and mid vowels are interchanged—the original high vowels become mid and the original vowels become high. Then the new mid vowels (i.e., the old high vowels) and the original low vowels interchange—the mid vowels become low and the low vowels become mid.

	ī	ē	æ	ɔ	ō	ū
Step I	ē	ī			ū	ō
Step II	æ		ē	ō		ɔ

Here are the two exchange rules, which are applied one after the other. Since the Vowel Shift does not apply to *ā*, these rules affect only segments which have the same values for the features [back] and [round].

Step I:
$$\begin{bmatrix} V \\ -\text{ low} \\ \alpha \text{ high} \\ \beta \text{ back} \\ \beta \text{ round} \\ +\text{ tense} \\ +\text{ stress} \end{bmatrix} \rightarrow [-\alpha \text{ high}]$$

Step II:
$$\begin{bmatrix} V \\ -\text{ high} \\ \alpha \text{ low} \\ \beta \text{ back} \\ \beta \text{ round} \\ +\text{ tense} \\ +\text{ stress} \end{bmatrix} \rightarrow [-\alpha \text{ low}]$$

These exchange rules are needed to account for synchronic alternations of the type *divine, divinity*; *serene, serenity*; *sane, sanity*. However, it is questionable whether the vowel shift as a historical phenomenon ever evolved in the way described by them.

Subscripts and Superscripts

When C_0 occurs in a rule the interpretation is "zero or more consonants." Any integer can appear as a *subscript* on a segment, and simply means that number of segments or more: e.g., C_1 means one or more consonants, C_2, two or more consonants, and so on. A subscript on a segment imposes a *lower bound* on the number of those segments needed for the rule to operate. To indicate an *upper bound*, *superscripts* are used. Thus, C_0^1 means zero or one consonant; C_0^2, between zero and two consonants; C_2^4, between two and four consonants; and so on. The upper bound restriction can be equivalently expressed through the parenthesis notation.

$$C_0^1 = (C), \quad C_0^2 = (C)(C), \quad C_1^2 = C(C)$$

If a segment contains a superscript but *no* subscript, the interpretation is "exactly that number of segments." Hence, C^1 means exactly one consonant and is equivalent to C; C^2, exactly two consonants and is equivalent to CC; and so on.

Notational Conventions Express
Linguistic Generalizations

The notational conventions employed in phonology are not to be regarded as abbreviatory tricks for saving space when writing rules. They are intended to capture relevant aspects of phonological processes. For example, C_0 is more than just a convenient way of saying zero or more consonants. Rather it reflects the important aspect of syllable structure that for some processes, such as the Germanic umlauting, the number of consonants separating vowels is irrelevant. On the other hand, there may be processes in which the number of consonants is significant. In the development from Latin to Italian, diphthongization occurred only with those stressed low vowels which were followed by no more than a single consonant. This consonantal restriction is captured by either C_0^1 or (C). The brace and parenthesis notations also make claims about how phonological processes operate—namely, that it is natural for a process to apply to strings which are partly identical and partly different. In French, word final consonants are deleted in phrase final position or whenever the next word begins with a consonant. Both deletions can be handled by the same rule, provided that ‖ and C are alternate environments. Another example where the notation reflects natural processes is the use of variables (the α notation). The variables become the formal means for recognizing that segments often take on values of (assimilate) features of neighboring segments.

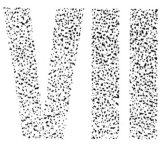

Underlying Representations

We have noted several times that the final consonant of the morpheme *electric* does not always have the same realization: electric versus electricity. It was suggested that the latter have as its abstract representation ⧣ elektrik + iti ⧣. But then we will need a phonological rule which converts k to s whenever the following morpheme begins with a nonlow front vowel.

$$⧣ \text{ elektrik} + \text{iti} ⧣$$

$k \rightarrow s$ ⧣ elektris + iti ⧣

vowel adjustments   əlektrisitīy

In this derivation we shall refer to ⧣ elektrik + iti ⧣ as the *underlying* (abstract) representation and to [əlektrisitīy] as the *derived* (phonetic) representation. To convert the former to the latter, in addition to changing k to s, the initial unstressed vowel has been reduced to schwa (vowel reduction), the final vowel has been made tense, and boundary symbols have been eliminated.

Why do we want all this machinery—underlying (abstract) representations, phonological rules, and derived (phonetic) representations?

1. The forms *pæs* (pass) and *pæk* (pack) constitute two separate morphemes which differ phonologically in the final consonant. The forms *əlektrik* and *əlektris* differ in the same way in their final consonants, yet they are variants of a single morpheme. We would like to show that at some level *əlektrik* and *əlektris* are somehow the same in a way in which *pæs* and *pæk* are not. If we have an underlying representation in which both alternants are represented identically, then we have given a unique representation to a unique morpheme.

2. The alternation *əlektrik, əlektris* is not limited to this one morpheme. Other morphemes exhibit the same consonant alternation: *fənætik* and *fənætis* in the words *fanatical* and *fanaticism.* The alternation between *k* and *s* is not random, but can be stated as a rule of English. Because the alternation is rule governed, an adequate description of English must indicate explicitly that this change occurs. It is the rules converting underlying representations to derived ones which explicitly characterize the processes of a language.

3. That the morpheme *electric* does in fact have two pronunciations, according to the surrounding environments, is a fact of life. At some point, we need to state all the ways in which a morpheme is phonetically realized. It is the derived representations which directly tell us the different phonetic manifestations of a morpheme.

Determining Underlying Representations

When one is working on a language for the first time and notes that morphemes exhibit phonological alternation that is rule governed, one must then determine the underlying or abstract representation of each morpheme, and the rules needed to derive all of that morpheme's variants from its unique underlying representation.

In French, many of the adjectives which appear before masculine nouns have two forms, one of which ends in a consonant, the other in a vowel.

pətit ami	little friend	pəti garsɔ̃	little boy
pətit ɔ̃kl	little uncle	pəti pɛr	little father
mešãt ãfã	naughty child	mešã garsɔ̃	naughty boy
groz ami	big friend	gro garsɔ̃	big boy
lɔ̃k ete	long summer	lɔ̃ prɛ̃tã	long spring

Whether the noun begins with a consonant or a vowel is the crucial environment for determining which variant of the adjective occurs. If we decide that the adjective form ending in a vowel is the underlying one, we need a rule to insert a final consonant before a word beginning with a vowel. Conversely, if we assume that the underlying form ends in a consonant, we need a rule which deletes that consonant before a word beginning with a consonant. The first alternative will not work, since we have no straightforward way of predicting which consonant should be inserted. In the examples shown, sometimes the final consonant is *t*, sometimes *z*, and sometimes *k*. On the other hand, if we choose the second alternative, where the underlying form of the adjective terminates in a consonant, we can derive the variant without the consonant by a simple rule of final consonant deletion.

$$C \rightarrow \emptyset / \underline{\quad\quad} \#C$$

Here are the derivations for 'little boy' and 'little friend'. Since boundary symbols do not appear in phonetic forms, they are erased as the last step in a derivation.

Underlying form	# pətit # garsɔ̃ #	# pətit # ami #
C deletion	# pəti # garsɔ̃ #	—
Derived form	pəti garsɔ̃	pətit ami

If we look elsewhere in French we find further evidence that a consonant is not inserted.

žɔli ãfã	pretty child	žɔli garsɔ̃	pretty boy

For [žɔ̃li ãfã] (unlike [pətit ãfã]), where the second vowel of the adjective is also *i*, there is no consonant before the word beginning with a vowel. Since the adjective 'pretty' never shows alternation, its underlying representation must terminate in a vowel, and would therefore never be subject to the consonant deletion rule.

French adjectives also have plural forms.

pətiz ami	little friends	pəti garsɔ̃	little boys
pətiz ɔ̃kl	little uncles	pəti pɛr	little fathers
mešãz ãfã	naughty children	mešã garsɔ̃	naughty boys
groz ami	big friends	gro garsɔ̃	big boys
lɔ̃z ete	long summers	lɔ̃ prɛ̃tã	long springs

Again we see that there are two variants, one ending in a vowel (note that the vowel forms are homophonous with the corresponding singulars), and the other in *z*, which, since it is a consonant, appears only before words beginning with a vowel. On the basis of the *z* forms, we deduce that *z* is the marker of the plural morpheme. As we already have a rule for deleting a consonant before a consonant, we can set up *z* as the plural marker for *all* forms. Now if the underlying representation of 'little' is *pətit*, then the plural form must be *pətit + z*, and the underlying representation for 'little boys' would have to be # pətit + z # garsɔ̃ #. However, the derived form, occurring phonetically, is [pəti garsɔ̃]. Therefore, we must delete both the final *t* of the morpheme *pətit* and the *z* marker. As the final *t* is no longer in word final position, the rule for final consonant deletion as given could not apply to this segment. But if we modify the rule so that it applies across either boundary symbol, we can account for all plural forms.

$$C \rightarrow \emptyset / \underline{\quad} \begin{Bmatrix} + \\ \# \end{Bmatrix} C$$

We give the derivations of 'little boys' and 'little friends'.

Underlying form	# pətit + z # garsɔ̃ #	# pətit + z # ami #
C deletion	# pəti # garsɔ̃ #	# pəti + z # ami #
Derived form	pəti garsɔ̃	pətiz ami

The deletion rule applies to all underlying segments which meet its conditions. For underlying # pətit + z # garsɔ̃ #, the final *t* and the plural *z* will both be deleted, since each precedes a boundary which is in turn followed by a consonant. In # pətit + z # ami #, only the final *t* fits the environment of boundary followed by a consonant.

We now see in what sense an underlying representation is abstract. It exhibits structural regularities which are not always apparent in the derived forms. In all forms, for example, the morpheme for 'little' has a consistent underlying representation wherever it occurs. Similarly the plural morpheme is a constituent of all plural forms, even though it may not always be phonetically realized. The phonological rules serve to explain the variants which appear. In French, it is the consonant deletion rule which accounts for the homophony of the singular and plural forms of adjectives before words beginning with a consonant, even though they have different underlying representations.

In German, there are alternations between voiced and voiceless obstruents.

bund*ə*	league (*dative*)	bun*t*	league (*nominative*)
tā*g*e	days	tā*k*	day
šter*b*ən	to die	štar*p*	died
glǣ*z*ər	glasses	glā*s*	glass

If the underlying forms contain a voiced segment, it has to become voiceless in word final position; on the other hand, if the underlying representations contain a voiceless obstruent, it would need to be made voiced in internal position. The second alternative does not hold for German, since voiceless obstruents appear internally. There are pairs such as:

bund*ə*	league (*dative*)	bun*t*	league (*nominative*)
bun*t*ə	colorful (*attributive*)	bun*t*	colorful (*predicative*)

Since there can be a contrast in medial position between voiced and voiceless obstruents (*bundə* versus *buntə*), this contrast has to be indicated in underlying representations; otherwise the forms could not be differentiated. What this means is that the morpheme 'league' has *bund* as its underlying representation, the morpheme 'colorful' has *bunt*, and there is a rule which devoices final obstruents. This rule accounts for the homophony of the morphemes *bund* and *bunt* when they occur as independent words.

	league (*nom.*)	league (*dat.*)	colorful (*pred.*)	colorful (*attrib.*)
Underlying form	# bund #	# bund + ə #	# bunt #	# bunt + ə #
C devoicing	# bunt #	—	—	—
Derived form	bunt	bundə	bunt	buntə

"More Abstract" Representations

For the alternations thus far presented, the underlying form is equivalent to one of the alternants. In French, where there is alternation between the presence and absence of a final consonant, the form with the consonant is set up as basic; in German, for the alternation between voiced and voiceless obstruents, the voiced one is underlying. There are cases where neither alternant can be set up as underlying, where all the alternants must be derived from an underlying form which coincides with none of them, and, hence, where the underlying form is even more abstract than those we have considered so far.

Yawelmani, a dialect of the Yokuts language of California, has verb forms containing a suffix *-it*.

xat*it*	eat
gop*it*	take care of an infant
giy*it*	touch
sa:p*it*	burn
go:b*it*	take in
me:k*ʔit*	swallow

There is a contrast between long and short vowels (*go:b* versus *gop*), which must be indicated in underlying representations. A type of vowel harmony affects certain suffix vowels in Yawelmani. If the stem vowel is *u* and the vowel of the suffix is a high vowel, as it is for *-it*, then the suffix vowel must also be *u*.

m*u*t*u*t	swear
h*u*d*u*t	recognize

We must posit a vowel harmony rule.

$$\begin{bmatrix} V \\ + \text{ high} \end{bmatrix} \rightarrow [+ \text{ round}]/ \begin{bmatrix} V \\ + \text{ high} \\ + \text{ round} \end{bmatrix} C_0 + C_0 \underline{\hspace{1cm}}$$

Here are the derivations for *go:bit* and *mutit*.

Underlying form	# go:b + it #	# mut + it #
Suffix harmony	—	# mut + ut #
Derived form	go:bit	mutut

Curiously, the *u* suffix vowel shows up after some stems containing long *o*.

ʔo:tʔut	steel
sudo:kʔut	remove

For other verbs, however, we have seen that the *i* suffix vowel appears after long *o* (e.g., *go:bit*). Thus, there are two kinds of *o:*—those which "behave" like *u* and cause the rounding of the suffix vowel, and those which "behave" normally. An examination of the surface vowels of Yawelmani reveals that only *e:*, *a:*, and *o:* occur as long vowels, but, strangely enough, long high vowels are lacking. Suffix harmony suggests that the underlying long vowel system is perhaps more normal, that long high vowels are needed, and that those occurrences of *o:* which behave like a high rounded vowel actually are derived from underlying *u:*. These long high vowels are not found in derived representations because at that level they have merged with the long mid vowels. Consequently, the underlying form for the stem 'steal' must be *ʔu:tʔ*, and we shall need a rule which lowers long high vowels. (An underlying short *u* is never lowered—e.g., the stem *mut*.)

$$
\begin{bmatrix} V \\ + \text{high} \\ + \text{long} \end{bmatrix} \rightarrow [- \text{high}]
$$

We give the derivations for *go:bit*, *mutut*, and *ʔo:tʔut*.

Underlying form	# go:b + it #	# mut + it #	# ʔu:tʔ + it #
Suffix harmony	—	# mut + ut #	# ʔu:tʔ + ut #
Long high V			
lowering	—	—	# ʔo:tʔ + ut #
Derived form	go:bit	mutut	ʔo:tʔut

Other phonological phenomena of Yawelmani support the positing of long high vowels in underlying representations. There is a class of bisyllabic verb stems with identical vowels, except that the first vowel is short and the second is long.

paxa:tit	mourn
yawa:lit	follow
ʔopo:tit	arise from bed

Other forms seem to be exceptions to the occurrence of identical vowels differing only in length.

> h*i*bey:it   bring water
> s*u*do:k ʔut   remove

These apparent exceptions contain a short high vowel in the first syllable and a long mid vowel in the second, when what we ought to find is a short high vowel in the first syllable and a long high vowel in the second. But we already know that long high vowels do not occur in derived representation in Yawelmani, and where we expect them we find instead long mid vowels. Once we recognize that although long high vowels do not appear in derived representations they *do* occur in underlying ones, forms such as *hibe:yit* and *sudo:k ʔut* will cease to be anomalies. The underlying representations of the stems are really *hibi:y* and *sudu:k*, both vowels now being identical except for length. The long high vowels will then be lowered by the rule given previously.

Underlying form	# hibi:y + it #	# sudu:kʔ + it #
Suffix harmony	—	# sudu:kʔ + ut #
Long high V lowering	# hibe:y + it #	# sudo:kʔ + ut #
Derived form	hibe:yit	sudo:k ʔut

The form *sudo:k ʔut* is particularly neat, since its underlying *u:* explains two different things. It accounts for the appearance of short *u* in the first syllable, where bisyllabic verb stems have identical vowels, and the occurrence of *u* in the suffix, where the vowel of *-it* becomes *u* whenever the preceding stem vowel is high rounded. What is interesting about the Yawelmani examples is that only by recognizing long high vowels, which never appear on the surface, are we able to account for phonological phenomena which at first appear to be irregular but which, *at the abstract level*, are shown to be instances of general processes operating in the language. This intriguing analysis of Yawelmani is due to Newman and Kuroda.

In English, there are alternations between stressed tense and lax vowels.

[āy]	[ĭ]
div*i*ne	div*i*nity
der*i*ve	der*i*vative
[īy]	[ĕ]
ser*e*ne	ser*e*nity
m*e*ter	m*e*trical
[ēy]	[æ]
s*a*ne	s*a*nity
prof*a*ne	prof*a*nity

Chomsky and Halle set up the following underlying representations for the stem morphemes: *divīn, derīv, serēn, mētr, sǣn, profǣn.* They show that the final vowel of the stem must be tense if one is to predict where stress falls in the above words. The stress is attracted to the right-most tense vowel. Further more, in English, an antepenultimate tense vowel becomes lax (trisyllabic laxing).

$$V \rightarrow [- \text{tense}]/\underline{\quad\quad} C_0VC_0VC_0 \;\#$$

This rule applies to the forms of the right-hand column above, causing the underlying tense vowel to become lax.

Underlying form	# divīn + iti #
Trisyllabic laxing	# divĭn + iti #
Other rules	dəvĭnətīy

For the forms of the left-hand column, the underlying vowels remain tense, since they are not antepenultimate. English tense vowels diphthongize: *ī → īy, ē → ēy, ǣ → ǣy.* The stressed tense vowels then undergo vowel shift: *ī* moves down to *ǣ, ǣ* moves up to *ē,* and *ē* moves up to *ī.* Finally, the vowel part of the diphthong *ǣy* becomes centralized, yielding *āy,* and the unstressed vowels are reduced. (See p. 58.)

Underlying form	# divīn #	# serēn #	# sǣn #
Diphthongization	# divīyn #	# serēyn #	# sǣyn #
Vowel shift	# divǣyn #	# serīyn #	# sēyn #
Centralization	# divāyn #	—	—
Vowel reduction	# dəvāyn #	# sərīyn #	—
Derived form	dəvāyn	sərīyn	sēyn

In this analysis, an underlying vowel does not coincide with any of its alternants. For example, underlying *ī* is manifested either as [ĭ] or [āy], but never does *ī* appear directly as such in any of its derived forms. However, the choice of *ī* as underlying these two variants is not arbitrary. First, it is undeniable that certain tense and lax vowels alternate, that there is a relationship between them. It is the quality (high frontness) of the abstract underlying vowel which in fact phonetically surfaces for the lax variant [ĭ]. Second, for the tense vowels, the quality of the glide (*y* or *w*) is predictable; front vowels take front glides, and rounded vowels round ones. Although the *y* of derived [āy] does not follow a front vowel, it does in the underlying representation, where the vowel is *ī.* (Only after diphthongization do the rules for vowel shift and centralization adjust the quality of that vowel.) Thus we can show that *ī* is an appropriate "link" for mediating between [ĭ] and [āy].

Suppletion

Whenever there are alternate forms of a morpheme, and rules can be stated for the occurrence of the alternants, the morpheme has a unique underlying representation. If the morpheme were not uniquely represented, then all its alternants would have to be separately listed in the lexicon along with a statement regarding their distribution. Such an approach would fail to recognize the systematic (rule-governed) nature of the alternation. But this is not to say that every alternation is systematic. Consider the present and past forms *go* and *went*. This alternation is found in no other pair of verbs and it follows from no general principles of English phonology. Since there is no way of predicting the alternation, both alternants have to be listed in the lexicon. Alternation which cannot be explained by any rule is known as *suppletion*.

What Does Abstractness Buy?

We have seen that underlying representations may be quite different from derived ones. Yet this difference is not to be had without cost. Each time an underlying representation "deviates" from the corresponding phonetic one, rules are required in order to return to the phonetic form, and, of course, as the underlying representation increases in "abstractness," the number of phonological rules will also increase. Consequently, there is little point in having abstract representations just for the sake of abstractness, because in each case one must show that the additional abstractness and the accompanying rules are *well motivated*—that they actually have a simplifying effect on the grammar.

Perhaps the most important simplifying effect is that in which morphemes show alternation, where there is a proliferation of variants on the surface. The lexicon will be simplified whenever a morpheme can have a single representation (excluding, of course, real cases of suppletion). Furthermore, rules accounting for the various alternants should not simply be devices for generating the appropriate derived forms, but rather ought to point to significant processes operating in the language. In other words, the rules should tell us a lot about how the language works.

Abstract representations also have an explanatory function. What on the surface may appear to be an irregularity or an anomaly often has an explanation at the abstract level. This was the case for Yawelmani, where underlying long high vowels explain the peculiar surface manifestation of suffix vowels and of vowels of bisyllabic verb stems. In French, all plural adjectives have the same structure in their underlying representations—they all contain the plural marker *z*—even though this marker does not always show up on the surface.

Similarities between Synchronic
and Diachronic Processes

The alternations occurring in a language are due to sound changes which took place in the history of that language. From historical evidence we know, for example, that at an earlier stage German had word final voiced obstruents. A sound change occurred which devoiced these segments, so that there arose alternations between voiced and voiceless obstruents within the morphology. Since the alternations found in any contemporary language are the vestiges of historical change, it should not be surprising that underlying representations often coincide with earlier attested forms, and that the synchronic phonological rules may (but not necessarily always) recapitulate the actual sound changes. Consequently, the historical changes which have occurred may continue to be *indirectly* reflected as phonological processes in the contemporary language. There is an interesting relationship between diachronic change and synchronic alternation, and a good deal of current research is concerned with this problem.

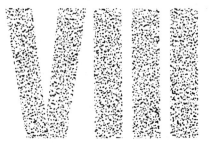

Ordered Rules

The phonological rules which map abstract underlying representations into derived surface representations frequently are *ordered*. In Yawelmani (p. 80), we saw that [sudo:kʔut] 'remove' is derived from an underlying ⧧ sudu:kʔ + it ⧧. Two rules are required: the suffix harmony rule, which causes a high suffix vowel to become *u* whenever the stem vowel is *u* (long or short), and the rule which lowers long high vowels, since *i*: and *u*: do not occur in derived representations. The derivation of [sudo:kʔut] shows that these rules must be applied in the order given.

Underlying form	⧧ sudu:kʔ + it ⧧
Suffix harmony	⧧ sudu:kʔ + ut ⧧
Long high V lowering	⧧ sudo:kʔ + ut ⧧
Derived form	sudo:kʔut

If long high vowels were lowered first, the vowel *u*: would no longer be present in the representation, and suffix harmony would not take place—*[sudo:kit].

Several rules may be ordered with respect to one another. In Yawelmani, long and short vowels contrast. However, before two or more consonants, distinctions in vowel length are neutralized. Only short vowels appear in this environment. We compare the passive aorist forms cited previously, where the suffix is *-it* or *-ut*, with the simple aorist forms, where the suffix is *-hin* or *-hun*.

Passive Aorist	Aorist	
xatit	xathin	eat
sa:pit	saphin	burn
gopit	gophin	take care of an infant
go:bit	gobhin	take in
mutut	muthun	swear
ʔo:tʔut	ʔotʔhun	steal

We need a rule which shortens vowels preceding two or more consonants. (Because a long vowel can appear before a consonant-glottal stop— ʔo:t ʔut— C ʔ is a unit segment, a glottalized consonant.)

$$V \rightarrow [- \text{long}]/\_\_\_C_2$$

Here is the derivation of the aorist [ʔot ʔhun].

Underlying form	⧺ ʔu:tʔ + hin ⧺
Suffix harmony	⧺ ʔu:tʔ + hun ⧺
Long high V lowering	⧺ ʔo:tʔ + hun ⧺
Vowel shortening	⧺ ʔotʔ + hun ⧺
Derived form	ʔotʔhun

All three rules are critically ordered. We already noted that long high vowel lowering has to follow suffix harmony. If *u:* were lowered first it would become *o:*, and the suffix vowel could not then become *u*. Vowel shortening has to follow long high vowel lowering. If *u:* were shortened first, it could not subsequently be lowered to *o*, since short vowels are never lowered.

Different Rule Orderings

One important way in which dialects can differ is in their rule ordering. Two dialects may have the same underlying forms and even the same rules, but the rules are applied in a different order. Certain derived forms will then be different. An interesting example of this phenomenon is found in English, where there is interaction between two rules: the rule which makes vowels (or the vowel part of a diphthong) long before voiced consonants (see p. 15), and the rule which converts intervocalic *t* and *d* to flap *D*.

$$V \rightarrow [+ \text{long}]/\_\_\_ \begin{bmatrix} C \\ + \text{voiced} \end{bmatrix}$$

$$\begin{Bmatrix} t \\ d \end{Bmatrix} \rightarrow D/V\_\_\_ \begin{bmatrix} V \\ - \text{stress} \end{bmatrix}$$

Notice that the flapping rule has been stated with segment symbols rather than with features, because in feature notation this rule is not very elegant. There is no problem in referring to *t* and *d* as a natural class; the difficulty resides in the feature specification for *D*. Do we really want to characterize it as a nonlateral liquid flap?

We derive the forms *write* [rāyt], *ride* [rā:yd], *writer* [rāyDər], and *rider* [rā:yDər]. (We ignore the representation of vowels in their pre-vowel shift condition.)

	write	*ride*	*writer*	*rider*
Underlying form	⫯ rāyt ⫯	⫯ rāyd ⫯	⫯ rāyt + ər ⫯	⫯ rāyd + ər ⫯
Vowel				
lengthening	—	⫯ rā:yd ⫯	—	⫯ rā:yd ⫯ ər ⫯
Flapping	—	—	⫯ rayD + ər ⫯	⫯ ra:yD + ər ⫯
Derived form	rāyt	rā:yd	rāyDər	rā:yDər

An interesting aspect of this derivation is that, in the underlying forms, *writer* and *rider* differ in the dental stop, whereas in the derived forms they differ in the length of the vowel.

If the rules are applied in the opposite order, *writer* and *rider* come out homophonous, which is the situation in some dialects of English.

	write	*ride*	*writer*	*rider*
Underlying form	⫯ rāyt ⫯	⫯ rāyd ⫯	⫯ rāyt + ər ⫯	⫯ rāyd + ər ⫯
Flapping	—	—	⫯ rāyD + ər ⫯	⫯ rāyD + ər ⫯
Vowel				
lengthening	—	⫯ rā:yd ⫯	⫯ rā:yD + ər ⫯	⫯ rā:yD + ər ⫯
Derived form	rāyt	rā:yd	rā:yDər	ra:yDər

A crucial property of ordered rules is that they apply or fail to apply to the most *recent* representation—that is, the output of one rule becomes the input to the next rule. In the case in which *writer* and *rider* are homophonous, the flapping rule merges *t* and *d* to *D*; the lengthening rule then applies to both forms, since *D phonetically* is a voiced segment. Of course, if some immediately preceding rules have failed to apply to a form, its most recent representation will be that resulting from the rule which last applied, or, in the event that no previous rules were applicable, it will be the underlying representation.

Kiparsky cites an example of Swiss German dialects differing in rule order. In these dialects the mid back vowel *o* is lowered to *ɔ* if it precedes a dental—so that *bodə* becomes *bɔdə*, whereas *bogə* stays as such. Furthermore, these nouns form their plurals by umlauting the first vowel.

In Dialect A the rules are applied in the order umlaut, lowering.

	Singular		Plural	
Underlying form	bodə	bogə	bodə	bogə
Umlaut (plural)	—	—	bödə	bögə
o → ɔ	bɔdə	—	—	—
Derived form	bɔdə	bogə	bödə	bögə

In Dialect B the plural of *bɔdə* is *bædə*, where the umlauted vowel is also low. In this dialect the lowering rule precedes umlaut.

	Singular		Plural	
Underlying form	bodə	bogə	bodə	bogə
o → ɔ	bɔdə	—	bɔdə	—
Umlaut (plural)	—	—	bœdə	bögə
Derived form	bɔdə	bogə	bœdə	bögə

FEEDING AND BLEEDING

Let us consider the number of words affected by the lengthening and flapping rules in English. For the sake of the discussion assume there is an equal number of items with intervocalic *t* and *d*. In the dialects which differentiate forms such as *writer* and *rider*—where voicing precedes flapping—the voicing rule applies to half the items (only those containing intervocalic *d*), whereas the flapping rule applies to all items. For those dialects exhibiting homophony—where flapping precedes voicing—both rules apply to all items precisely because the first rule, flapping, changes intervocalic voiceless *t* to voiced *D*, which creates an environment for the second rule, lengthening. *Feeding order* is that in which the output of one rule (for example, flapping) *increases* the number of items to which the second rule (lengthening) is applicable. On the other hand, should the output of the first rule *decrease* the number of items to which the second rule can apply, we have *bleeding order*. In Swiss German dialect B the lowering rule applies to both the singular and plural of *bodə*. In dialect A the lowering rule applies only to the singular, since the umlaut rule, which applies first, changes *o* to *ö*, making *o* no longer available for lowering. Consequently, in Dialect A the rules are in a bleeding relationship. Kiparsky has claimed that rule application tends to be maximized—that is, rules should apply to as many forms as possible. According to this hypothesis, when a language or dialect undergoes rule reordering, rules will tend to establish themselves in a feeding order.

Partial Ordering

We have presented several examples of ordered rules. Two rules are ordered if, for some forms, applying the rules in one order results in a different output from applying them in a different order. If all orders lead to the same derived forms, then the rules are not really ordered. For example, English vowels contiguous to nasal consonants are phonetically nasalized. In addition, vowels become long before voiced consonants. If a vowel precedes a nasal consonant, both rules apply, since a nasal consonant is also a voiced consonant. However, these two rules are not ordered: whichever order is taken, the resulting vowels are always long and nasalized. Of course, in giving a list of rules we are forced to place some rules before others, but this should not be confused with the technical sense of ordered rules. Actually, then, phonological rules are only *partially ordered*.

Unordered versus Ordered Rules

A set of ordered rules, whether totally ordered or partially ordered, can always be replaced by *unordered* ones, provided the full set of unordered rules is thought of as applying *simultaneously* to the underlying representation. However, such rules are invariably more complex. For example, if we were to abandon ordered rules, we would need three rules, instead of two, to account for those dialects in which *writer* and *rider* are homophonous.

$$V \rightarrow [+ \text{ long}]/\underline{\quad} \begin{bmatrix} C \\ + \text{ voiced} \end{bmatrix}$$

$$V \rightarrow [+ \text{ long}]/\underline{\quad} t \begin{bmatrix} V \\ - \text{ stress} \end{bmatrix}$$

$$\begin{Bmatrix} t \\ d \end{Bmatrix} \rightarrow D/V\underline{\quad} \begin{bmatrix} V \\ - \text{ stress} \end{bmatrix}$$

The first lengthening rule affects the vowels of *ride* and *rider*, and the second lengthening rule the vowel of *writer*. But the environment for the second rule is nearly identical to the environment required for the third rule, the flapping rule. Imposing an ordering on rules makes it possible to simplify their environments, particularly in terms of stating similar environmental conditions only once, and therefore to capture generalizations operating within the phonology. Worse yet, the unordered rules fail to explain why lengthening should occur in *writer*. There is a special rule needed to lengthen vowels preceding *t* and an unstressed vowel, which is, by itself, a somewhat strange environment for vowel lengthening. With ordered rules, this peculiar environment is eliminated entirely, and the lengthening is a consequence of the interaction of two general processes of English which need to be recognized in any case. The flapping rule applies first, converting the voiceless stop of *writer* to a voiced flap. The vowel can subsequently undergo lengthening since it now precedes a voiced segment. What is important about ordering, then, is not just that it allows us to eliminate environments in rules, but rather that the environments which are eliminated are very often highly suspicious. This is one of the strongest arguments for ordered rules.

Disjunctive Ordering

For French words spoken in isolation, the stress is either on the penultimate or the final syllable. If the vowel of the final syllable is schwa, the stress is on the penultimate: [admiráblə] 'admirable', [pətítə] 'little' (*feminine*); otherwise the final vowel bears the stress: [amí] 'friend', [garsɔ́] 'boy'.

$$V \rightarrow [+ \text{ stress}]/\_\_\_C_0 \begin{bmatrix} V \\ - \text{ tense} \end{bmatrix} \#$$

$$V \rightarrow [+ \text{ stress}]/\_\_\_C_0 \#$$

The rules must be applied in this order. If the second rule preceded the first, then every word, including those with final schwa, would receive final stress, which the second rule assigns indiscriminately. But it is not sufficient that the first rule precede the second. Their application must also be *mutually exclusive*. If the first rule applies—*admiráblə*—then the second rule cannot. If it did, some words would incorrectly receive two stresses—**admiráblɔ́*. Therefore, for the two stress rules of French, we must impose the constraint that application of the first rule blocks application of the second. (Obviously, if the first rule does not apply because there is no final schwa—*ami*—then the second rule does apply—*amí*.) This constraint on ordering is known as *disjunctive ordering*: ordered rules are treated as if they were mutually exclusive, in spite of the fact that later rules meet the environmental conditions for application. Thus, in the case of disjunctively ordered rules, in the derivation of any one form, only one rule out of the ordered set (the first one applicable) will ever apply.

Disjunctive ordering is not a constraint that we want to impose on *all* ordered rules, for we have seen cases of ordered rules, such as the vowel lengthening and flapping rules of English, where we want both rules to apply to the same form in the course of its derivation. Hence, only some ordered rules are disjunctively ordered, and it becomes important to find some formal means for identifying rules which have this property. In the discussion of rules in Chapter 6, we noted that the stress facts of French can be stated as a single rule through the parenthesis notation.

$$V \rightarrow [+ \text{ stress}]/\_\_\_C_0 \left(\begin{bmatrix} V \\ - \text{ tense} \end{bmatrix} \right) \#$$

This suggests that parentheses are the appropriate formalism for showing disjunctive ordering, on condition that the parenthesized rule is interpreted as follows: First see whether the longer environment (i.e., with the parenthesized element included) fits the situation. Only if it does not should you then see whether the shorter environment is applicable.

Conjunctive Ordering

In French, a consonant can be deleted when it is followed by a morpheme boundary and a following consonant or a word boundary and a following consonant.

$$C \rightarrow \emptyset / \underline{\hspace{1cm}} + C$$

$$C \rightarrow \emptyset / \underline{\hspace{1cm}} \# C$$

In Chapter 7 we saw that the plural form [pəti garsɔ̃] 'little boys' is derived from an underlying # pətit + z # garsɔ̃ #. Both the final *t* of *pətit* and the plural marker *z* have to be deleted, which means that both rules apply to this form. Furthermore, the rules are ordered: The deletion of a consonant before the + boundary precedes the deletion before the # boundary. If the *z* of # pətit + z # garsɔ̃ # were deleted first, there would no longer be a consonant following the + boundary and the final *t* could not be deleted. Because both rules apply in the same derivation they are *not* disjunctively ordered. Furthermore, the rules cannot be collapsed through the parenthesis notation, although they can be collapsed with braces.

$$C \rightarrow \emptyset / \underline{\hspace{1cm}} \begin{Bmatrix} + \\ \# \end{Bmatrix} C$$

In interpreting braces, we must allow both subparts of the rule to apply, a process known as *conjunctive ordering*: The subparts of the rule are ordered; if one of the subparts applies, the remaining ones are *not* skipped but also apply if the appropriate conditions are met.

The Steps in a Derivation

A phonology of a natural language would usually have a considerable number of rules, many of which would have to be ordered. It is the total set of rules which converts underlying representations to derived representations. If the first rule applies to the underlying representation, that representation is changed in some way. The second rule applies or fails to apply to the changed representation (or to the underlying representation, in the event that the first rule did not apply). If the second rule applies, the representation is further changed, and so on, so that the output of one rule always becomes the input to the next. After application of the last rule, one arrives at the final derived representation. Between the underlying and the derived representations, there may be many intermediate representations, one for each of the rules which applies to the form in question. These intermediate forms are not of any great theoretical interest. Of the many representations which can occur in a derivation, the important ones are the first and the last—the *underlying* and the *derived.*

Additional Similarities between Synchronic and Diachronic Processes

At the conclusion of the preceding chapter we observed that the underlying forms in the contemporary language frequently coincide with earlier attested forms for that language, and that the synchronic phonological rules may correlate with diachronic sound changes. There is a further interesting parallel. Because phonological rules are ordered, the ordering established in the synchronic language may recapitulate the chronological order of the sound changes. As a result of these correlations between a synchronic description and historical evolution, a description of a contemporary language often enables one to make intelligent guesses about its history—what earlier forms were, which sound changes occurred, and the order in which they appeared. However, this internal reconstruction is only approximate, since the parallelisms between synchrony and diachrony are not perfect.

    1. Because the alternations in the contemporary language are vestiges of historical change, this evidence of the change would cease to exist if the alternation disappeared. If the few irregular plurals in English, such as *foot, feet* were to become regular—*foot, foots*—there would no longer be evidence that umlauting had occurred in the history of the language.

    2. Alternations occur only where a sound change happens in some environments, but not others. If a sound changes in all environments there are no alternations, since the old sound no longer exists and is replaced everywhere by the new one. Consequently, a synchronic description might provide no evidence of the earlier sound.

3. In a synchronic description rules are partially ordered. Those rules which are not critically ordered may shed little light on chronological order.

4. One way in which dialects can differ is through rule ordering. Reordering of rules is one type of language change. Consequently, although a set of ordered rules often reflects the correct chronological order, it will not coincide with the synchronic order if rule reordering has occurred.

5. A rule is often generalized to cover forms not originally affected. In French, word final schwas were at first deleted only when the next word began with a vowel. Today, in colloquial speech, nearly all word final schwas are dropped. Consequently, a synchronic rule may not be historically accurate.

6. Conversely, the synchronic rule may be less general than the original change. In French, vowels were nasalized before a nasal consonant. They were subsequently denasalized when the nasal consonant was followed by a vowel. The synchronic rule states that vowel nasalization takes place when the nasal consonant is followed by another consonant or by a pause. Consequently, a diachronic rule may be simpler than a synchronic one.

7. Several changes may converge so that they can be expressed most simply in a synchronic grammar as a single rule. It is questionable whether the exchange rule accounting for the vowel shifts in contemporary English reflects the actual diachronic progression. Hence, an elegant synchronic rule may be historically inaccurate.

Derived Representations

Phonological rules apply to underlying representations and convert them to other representations. We have not yet considered exactly how this operation is performed. Recall that within the lexicon morphemes are represented as sequences of bundles of distinctive features. The two morphemes of German, *bund* and *bunt*, have the following underlying representations when they occur as independent words.

	#	b	u	n	d	#	#	b	u	n	t	#
Syllabic		−	+	−	−			−	+	−	−	
Sonorant		−	+	+	−			−	+	+	−	
Consonantal		+	−	+	+			+	−	+	+	
Continuant		−			−			−			−	
Delayed release		−			−			−			−	
Nasal			−	+					−	+		
Anterior		+		+	+			+		+	+	
Coronal		−		+	+			−		+	+	
High		−	+	−	−			−	+	−	−	
Low		−	−	−	−			−	−	−	−	
Back		−	+	−	−			−	+	−	−	
Round		−	+	−	−			−	+	−	−	
Voiced		+	+	+	+			+	+	+	−	

To these forms is applied the rule for devoicing voiced obstruents in word final position.

$$\begin{bmatrix} - \text{ sonorant} \\ + \text{ voiced} \end{bmatrix} \rightarrow [- \text{ voiced}]/\underline{\quad} \#$$

In order for a rule to apply to a segment, that segment must contain all of the feature values mentioned to the left of the arrow. It may, of course, contain additional feature specifications not relevant for that rule. In addition, any environmental conditions must be met. Thus, the devoicing rule will apply to # bund # since the final *d* has among its specifications [− sonorant, + voiced] and is followed by a word boundary. The rule will not apply to the *t* of # bunt # as it does not contain the specification [+ voiced], nor will it apply to the initial *b* of either # bund # or # bunt #, for although initial *b* contains the specifications to the left of the arrow, it fails to fulfil the environmental constraint. If a segment meets all the required conditions, all feature values mentioned to the right of the arrow are then changed. In the matrix for # bund # the [+ voiced] specification for *d* will be changed to [− voiced], making the matrix identical to that for # bunt #.

Vacuous Rule Application

In the German devoicing rule, the feature which changes value in the right half of the rule is mentioned on the left. In actuality, the left half can be simplified by dispensing with the [+ voiced] specification.

$$[- \text{sonorant}] \rightarrow [- \text{voiced}]/\underline{\hspace{2em}} \#$$

This rule now applies to all obstruents instead of just voiced ones. The final *d* of # bund # meets the required conditions, as its matrix contains the specification [− sonorant], and since the value for voicing must be −, the original [+ voiced] specification will be changed. In the case of # bunt #, the final *t* will also meet the conditions of the rule. But since this obstruent is [− voiced] to begin with, the rule really has no effect on this segment. If the rule applies, it applies *vacuously*.

Rules are usually written in their most general form, so that many rules will have vacuous application for some segments. This vacuity should not be regarded as a notational trick for using fewer features in writing rules. The resulting rules frequently capture generalizations about derived representations. Our revised rule, for example, states that in derived representations the word final obstruents of German are always voiceless.

Presence or Absence of Plus in a Rule

If a rule mentions a boundary as part of the environment, then that boundary must be present in the underlying representation in order for the rule to be applicable to the segment. Thus, the German devoicing rule applies only to those obstruents immediately followed by the $\#$ boundary. Consider the rule converting k to s when the following morpheme begins with a nonlow front vowel

$$\begin{bmatrix} - \text{ delayed release} \\ - \text{ anterior} \\ - \text{ voiced} \end{bmatrix} \rightarrow \begin{bmatrix} + \text{ strident} \\ + \text{ anterior} \\ + \text{ coronal} \end{bmatrix} / \underline{\quad} + \begin{bmatrix} \text{V} \\ - \text{ low} \\ - \text{ back} \end{bmatrix}$$

This change does not take place where the k is not followed by a morpheme boundary, as in *keep, kill, Kent*. Consequently, a rule which has a $+$ boundary can apply *only* to those forms where there is a morpheme boundary at the place indicated by the $+$.

Yet there are rules which apply both within a single morpheme and across morphemes; the English flapping rule is such. This rule applies to words containing only one morpheme, such as *water* or *capital* or *spider*. Therefore, no $+$ boundary is mentioned in the rule.

$$\left. \begin{matrix} t \\ d \end{matrix} \right\} \rightarrow \text{D} / \text{V} \underline{\quad} \begin{bmatrix} \text{V} \\ - \text{ stress} \end{bmatrix}$$

Flapping also applies to the t and d of *writ+er* and *rid+er*, where the unstressed vowel belongs to a separate morpheme. Obviously, we do not want two separate flapping rules. It happens almost without exception that rules affecting a sequence of segments within a single morpheme also apply to the same sequence distributed in separate morphemes. Therefore, there is a convention within generative phonology that a rule not specifically mentioning a $+$ between segments *nonetheless applies to segments separated by a morpheme boundary*.

Multivalued Features

At the systematic phonetic level we must be able not only to specify the allophones of a language, but also to characterize phonetic differences between languages. For example, at the phonetic level, English and Korean both have stops specified as [$+$ aspirated]. Those in Korean are strongly aspirated, whereas those in English are only moderately aspirated. Since it is linguistically significant that language differ in the details of their phonetics, a requirement of phonetic representations is that there be some way of showing small degrees of differences in the actual phonetic realizations of features. It should be evident that a binary system is inadequate for capturing any degree of fine phonetic detail. All we can do within such a system is indicate whether or not an attribute is present; we cannot show *how much* of it is there.

Suppose we were to recognize four degrees of aspiration: 0, unaspirated; 1, weakly aspirated; 2, moderately aspirated; and 3, strongly aspirated. In both English and Korean, segments specified as [− aspirated] are of course [0 aspirated]. However, segments specified as [+ aspirated] will have different phonetic values in the two languages: [2 aspirated] in English, [3 aspirated] in Korean. We can now account for fine phonetic differences between languages, or even between allophones within the same language, once we allow a single binary value to be mapped into several scalar ones.

$$[- \text{ aspirated}] \rightarrow [0 \text{ aspirated}]$$

$$[1 \text{ aspirated}]$$
$$\nearrow$$
$$[+ \text{ aspirated}] \rightarrow [2 \text{ aspirated}]$$
$$\searrow$$
$$[3 \text{ aspirated}]$$

Comparing the Phonological
Inventories of Languages

There are two levels at which we can compare segments across languages: the abstract and the phonetic. At the abstract level, the values of features are binary. Because we are interested in knowing which features of sound can differentiate forms, and not in how much of the feature is actually there, binary values are ideal for indicating whether or not an attribute is present. At this level we want to state, for example, that a language has vowels which are opposed in rounding, or that it makes use of aspiration contrastively. As we are not concerned with the absolute phonetic qualites of segments, but only with the relative differences between them *in any one language system*, we can have identical feature specifications for segments in different languages, even though they may not be phonetically implemented in the same way.

At the phonetic level, we want to give a precise account of the phonetic properties of segments. We want to know how similar type segments are realized for different languages, and the subtle differences between them. Within the same language, we want to determine by which features and to what degree allophones differ. To arrive at such detailed transcriptions, the binary values may need to be reinterpreted as multivalued ones.

Taxonomic Phonemes
and Systematic Phonemes

We are now ready to return to the controversy between taxonomic phonemes and systematic phonemes (see p. 7). What generative phonologists call *taxonomic phonemes*, or autonomous phonemes, are those segments which *contrast on the surface*. For example, in Yawelmani, there would be three "phonemic" long vowels—*e:*, *a:*, and *o:*—since, on the surface, these are the only long vowels which can contrast with one another. Yet we have seen that the under-lying vowel system contains long high vowels which are needed to explain such phenomena as suffix harmony or the occurrence of identical vowels differing in length in bisyllabic verb stems. Because of the different inventories of abstract underlying segments and of those segments which can contrast on the surface, a taxonomic phonemic representation cannot usually be equated with an under-lying one. What we have been calling an underlying representation is frequently referred to by generative phonologists as a *systematic phonemic* (as opposed to a taxonomic phonemic) representation.

If there is any relationship between systematic phonemic and taxonomic phonemic, it is the following: A systematic phonemic representation will be equivalent to a taxonomic phonemic one unless there is good reason to deviate from the latter. Morphological alternations or pattern congruities lacking in a taxonomic phonemic representation are good reasons for positing a more abstract representation. For example, the systematic phonemic (underlying) representation for the word *pass* would be *pæs*, which is equivalent to a taxo-nomic phonemic representation, but the systematic phonemic representation for the stem part of *electricity* would be *elektrik*, and not the taxonomic phonemic /elektris/, as there is morphological evidence for deriving some occurrences of *s* from *k*.

Most generative phonologists recognize only systematic phonemes. Furthermore, they claim that the taxonomic phonemes of structural linguistics are not relevant entities within a total phonological description. They argue that the complete set of phonological rules converts underlying abstract (systematic phonemic) representations into derived surface (systematic phonetic) representations. The most general set of rules directly relates these two levels, and in the course of a derivation there is no intermediate represen-tation unequivocally correlated with the taxonomic phonemic. Therefore, a taxonomic phonemic representation is unmotivated. Q.E.D. But there is a relationship between derived and taxonomic phonemic representations which has been completely overlooked in generative phonology.

A *systematic phonetic* representation is, in theory, one in which the features are specified with integer values. Although, ideally, all derivations should end with precise phonetic specifications, those we have given, as well as those appearing in nearly all published generative descriptions, stop far short of this detail. This is because generative phonology has concentrated primarily on the nature of underlying representations and on morphemes exhibiting phonological alternation, and accordingly there has been much less concern with fine phonetic differences. Interestingly, these derived representations are amazingly similar to taxonomic phonemic representations, precisely because the phonological rules found in the literature map abstract underlying segments specified with binary features into less abstract surface segments also specified with binary features, segments which contrast on the surface. This similarity between "quasi-abstract" derived representations and traditional taxonomic phonemic representations has not been appreciated in current generative phonological discussions.

Relationship between Systematic Phonemic and Systematic Phonetic Segments

Generative phonology claims that the same set of universal features characterizes segments at both the systematic phonemic and systematic phonetic levels. The only difference is that whereas the values for those features are always binary at the systematic phonemic level, they may be multivalued at the systematic phonetic. This means that underlying (systematic phonemic) representations have "phonetic" content even though they are not necessarily "pronounceable" as such in the language. But do we have the right to claim, for example, that in Yawelmani [sudo:k ʔut] has *sudu:k ʔ* as the systematic phonemic representation of the stem when a long high vowel is never pronounceable in this language?

Since the systematic phonemic representations are *abstract* (unique representations for morphemes showing variation on the surface), why not use abstract symbols divorced from phonetics—for example, *sud*k ʔ*? Such representations would show explicitly that the abstract vowel is not pronounceable as such. Of course, ultimately we would need a pronunciation rule: * → o:. This is precisely the approach frequently found in the morphophonemic descriptions of certain nongenerative phonologies.

Notice what such a view entails. First, we are required to state that bisyllabic verb stems containing * have *u* as the first vowel of the stem and take the *ü* suffix vowel. Furthermore, we still need rules stating that for stems not containing *—with "real" vowels—the first vowel is a shortened version of the second (*paxa:tit, ʔopo:tit*), and the *u* suffix vowel appears only when the stem vowel is high back rounded (*mutut, hudut*). Whereas the rules for the "real" vowels are phonologically motivated, the rules for * have little rhyme or reason. Why should * require a preceding short *u* and govern the *u* suffix vowel? Precisely because * is *functioning* like *u:*, so why pretend otherwise? Once we recognize that * is "really" *u:*, everything affected by this "unreal" vowel is a consequence of processes independently required for the "real" vowels.

The second point is that although we can motivate *u:*, there is still a cost, for eventually we will need a pronunciation (?) rule: *u:* → *o:*. Yet there is a tremendous difference between the complexity of this rule and of the other rule: * → *o:*. The latter requires that * be replaced by the full set of features needed to specify *o:*, while the conversion of *u:* to *o:* is a one feature change: [+ high] becomes [− high], with all other feature values staying intact. So there is a "simplicity" argument at stake.

The third point is that although underlying representations may "deviate" from the phonetics, it is really not by very much. If we compare underlying |sudu:k?+it| with derived [sudo:k?ut], only two of the seven segments are different. Thus most of the time there is a direct correlation between underlying (abstract) segments and derived (phonetic) segments. (There will of course have to be allophonic specifications for the latter, but these are needed in anybody's phonology.)

To sum up, any approach which ignores the fact that abstract (systematic phonemic) representations contain features with "real" phonetic content fails to recognize that there is usually a direct correlation (excluding allophonic statements) between underlying and derived forms, that where they differ they differ minimally, and, most important, that the abstract entities actually *function* as *natural classes* which are *phonetically definable*.

Nonphonological Effects

For the majority of rules we have given, either the phonological change was unconditional—that is, it took place everywhere—or else it occurred only in certain environments. The environments were stated in terms of surrounding segments and boundaries. We did not have to consider nonphonological properties of forms—for example, whether they were stems, verbs, or noun phrases. However, there are cases where such information is required.

Syntactic Categorization

In English, compounds and phrases have different stress contours. For compounds composed of two words, the main or primary stress is on the first word, while the second word has a weaker or secondary stress. On the other hand, the primary stress for phrases is on the second word, while the first word has the secondary.

Compound Nouns		Noun Phrases	
1　　2 blackbird	(a certain species of bird)	2　　1 black bird	(any bird which is black)
1　　2 bird's-nest	(a type of nest)	2　　1 bird's nest	(a nest belonging to a bird)

Compound Nouns		Noun Phrases	

¹ ²		² ¹	
White House	(the President's domicile)	white house	(any house which is white)
¹ ²		² ¹	
French teacher	(one who teaches French)	French teacher	(a teacher of French nationality)

Compound Verbs	Verb Phrases

¹ ²	² ¹
to pickpocket	to pick pockets
¹ ²	² ¹
to typewrite	to type right
¹ ²	² ¹
to proofread	to read proof

Taking the forms *blackbird* and *black bird* as typical examples of compounds and phrases, we note that they are composed of the same two words, the adjective *black* and the noun *bird*. The following tree diagrams show that when these two words are combined, they are labeled differently according to their syntactic constituent structure. *A*, *N*, and *NP* stand for adjective, noun, and noun phrase, respectively. Compound nouns are labeled *N* since their syntactic behavior resembles that of ordinary nouns.

English words in isolation contain one primary stress. If the word is monosyllabic, then of course its only vowel receives the primary stress. Thus,
¹   ¹
black and *bird* as separate words each have a primary stress. When the two words are combined into a compound or a phrase, only one of the primary stresses is retained; the other is reduced to secondary. We can informally state rules for deriving the stress contours of compounds and phrases.

    I: **In compounds, the left-most primary stress is retained; other stresses are weakened.**

    II: **In phrases, the right-most primary stress is retained; other stresses are weakened.**

When *black bird* is labeled *N*, the compound rule converts it to *black bird*; when it is labeled *NP*, the phrase rule converts it to *black bird*. In derivations parentheses are normally used for showing constituent structure.

	(black	bird)$_N$	(black	bird)$_{NP}$
Word stress	1	1	1	1
Compound rule	1	2		
Phrase rule			2	1

Compounds and phrases can be embedded within one another, producing intricate stress contours exemplifying more than two degrees of stress.

black bird's-nest	a bird's-nest which is black
blackbird's nest	the nest of a blackbird
black bird's nest	the nest of a bird which is black

These three phrases all have different syntactic analyses, as shown in the diagrams below.

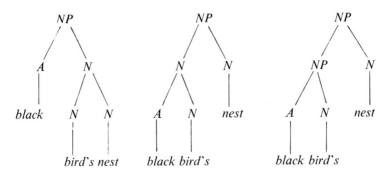

The stress relations follow from what we already know regarding stress assignment in compounds and phrases. In the first example, the adjective *black* modifies the compound *bird's-nest*. The latter by itself has the stress contour 1-2, and *black* has its own primary stress: (black (bird's nest)$_N$)$_{NP}$. The whole construction is a noun phrase—*black bird's-nest* is like *black car*. For phrases the right-most primary stress is retained, which in this case is the one on *bird's*. The other stresses have to be weakened. The primary stress on *black* becomes secondary, and the secondary stress on *nest* becomes tertiary: *black bird's nest*.

(black (bird's nest)$_N$)$_{NP}$

Word stress	1	1	1
Compound stress		1	2
Phrase stress	2	1	3

In an analogous fashion we can derive the stress contours of the other two examples.

THE PHONOLOGICAL CYCLE

The preceding examples show that the stress contour of a larger unit can be completely predicted from the structure of the smaller constituents of which it is composed. That is, the rules which assign stress to larger units are precisely the same as those which assign stress to smaller units. A system of this type is known as a *cycle*. Cyclic rules have three essential properties: (1) The rules make reference to syntactic categorization. (2) The entire set of rules can be applied more than once. (3) The manner in which the rules are applied in each cycle is determined by the size of the syntactic units—the rules apply to increasingly larger syntactic constructions.

We derive the stress contour of *Spanish American history teacher*, i.e., a teacher of the history of America who is of Spanish nationality. The first constituent above the word level is the noun phrase *American history*. This phrase is combined with the noun *teacher*, yielding a still larger unit, the compound noun *American history teacher*. In English, when a subject title precedes words such as *teacher* or *professor*, the construction functions as a compound— *French teacher*, *physics professor*. Finally, the compound *American history teacher* is combined with the adjective *Spanish*, giving the largest unit, which is a noun phrase. Above the word level there are three cycles.

(Spanish ((American history)$_{NP}$teacher)$_N$)$_{NP}$

Word stress	1	1	1	1
Cycle 1: Phrase stress		2	1	
Cycle 2: Compound stress		3	1	2
Cycle 3: Phrase stress	2	4	1	3

The first cycle applies to the smallest constituent: (American history)$_{NP}$. Since it is a phrase, the right-most primary stress is retained and the other stress weakened: *American history*. The second cycle applies to the next larger unit:

$$\overset{2}{\text{(American}} \overset{1}{\text{history}} \overset{1}{\text{teacher)}_N}.$$ As it is a compound, the left-most primary stress is retained and all other stresses are weakened: $\overset{3}{American} \overset{1}{history} \overset{2}{teacher}$. Finally, the rules apply to the largest constituent: $\overset{1}{\text{(Spanish}} \overset{3}{\text{American}} \overset{1}{\text{history}}$ $\overset{2}{\text{teacher)}_{NP}}.$ Because this is a phrase, the right-most primary stress is kept; all other stresses are weakened: $\overset{2}{Spanish} \overset{4}{American} \overset{1}{history} \overset{3}{teacher}$. The cyclic analysis of English stress is taken from Chomsky and Halle.

Diacritic Features

SYNTACTIC FEATURES

Certain phonological processes take place, for example, only in certain verb tenses or in the plural. In Spanish, verbs in some tenses take penultimate stress. We cite the present indicative and subjunctive of the verb "to sing". (The stressed vowel is the italicized one.)

Present Indicative		Present Subjunctive	
k*a*nt + o	kant + *a* + mos	k*a*nt + e	kant + *e* + mos
k*a*nt + a + s	kant + *a* + is	k*a*nt + e + s	kant + *e* + is
k*a*nt + a	k*a*nt + a + n	k*a*nt + e	k*a*nt + e + n

In the imperfect indicative and subjunctive, the first and second persons plural receive antepenultimate stress.

Imperfect Indicative

kant + *a* + ba	kant + *a* + ba + mos
kant + *a* + ba + s	kant + *a* + ba + is
kant + *a* + ba	kant + *a* + ba + n

Imperfect Subjunctive

kant + *a* + ra	kant + *a* + ra + mos
kant + *a* + ra + s	kant + *a* + ra + is
kant + *a* + ra	kant + *a* + ra + n

In all forms of the imperfect the stress is on the conjugation vowel *a*, the vowel immediately following the verb stem. The stress rule for Spanish must state that for verbs the vowel after the stem is stressed in the imperfect tense forms, while in other tenses it is the penultimate vowel which bears the stress. How can we refer to notions such as *imperfect tense* in phonological rules?

A form such as *kantaba* '(he) was singing' would not appear as such in the lexicon. Instead, the lexicon would contain the stem element *kant* 'sing'. The lexicon lists different kinds of information about this stem—phonological information, e.g., that it is composed of four segments, that the first segment is *k*; morphological information, e.g., that it belongs to the first conjugation; syntactic information, e.g., that it is a verb, that it occurs with animate subjects; and semantic information, i.e., its various meanings and uses.

Morphological and syntactic properties can also be represented as binary features—for example, [+ plural] and [− plural] for *plural* and *singular*; [+ subjunctive] and [− subjunctive] for *subjunctive* and *indicative*; [+ 1 conjugation] for *first conjugation*.

A sentence such as *Pedro cantaba ayer* 'Pedro was singing yesterday' can be schematized as follows. (A detailed feature specification for each lexical item is obviously not given.)

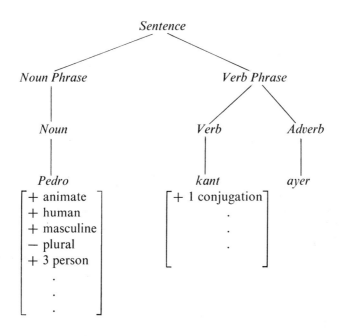

The syntactic component of the grammar would indicate that the verb must be made imperfect indicative—that is, the features [+ past, − perfect,

— subjunctive] are to be added to the set of features contained in the verb stem. There is also a syntactic rule stating that a verb must agree with its subject in person and number. These features would be copied from the noun into the verb stem. After these syntactic rules have applied, we obtain the following structure:

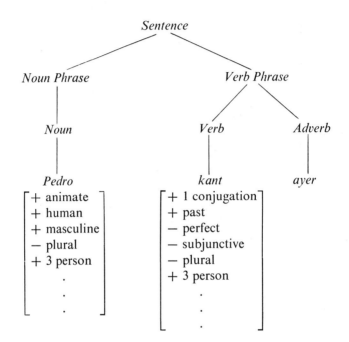

Prior to the application of the phonological rules there would be a set of *segmentalization rules*, whose function is to translate certain syntactic and morphological features into a string of segments—the inflectional endings—to be added to the verb stem. These rules would state, for example, that the inflectional morphemes include a conjugation vowel, a tense marker, and a person-number ending, which are added to the verb stem in this order. Furthermore, they would indicate that when the verb stem is marked [+ 1 conjugation] the conjugation vowel is *a*, when the verb stem is marked [+ 1 conjugation, + past, − perfect, − subjunctive] the tense marker is *ba*, and when the stem is marked [+ 3 person, − plural] there is no overt manifestation of a person-number ending. Word boundaries are then placed at the beginning and end of the string and the whole word bears the same syntactic categorization which dominates the stem. After these operations we arrive at the form:

$$[\# \ [\text{kant}]_{\text{Verb}} \qquad + a + ba \ \#]_{\text{Verb}}$$

$$\begin{bmatrix} + \ 1 \ \text{conjugation} \\ + \ \text{past} \\ - \ \text{perfect} \\ - \ \text{subjunctive} \\ - \ \text{plural} \\ + \ 3 \ \text{person} \\ \quad \cdot \\ \quad \cdot \\ \quad \cdot \end{bmatrix}$$

This becomes the underlying representation to which the phonological rules are applied. (Although segmentalization rules permit us to handle more or less effectively the concatenation and ordering of inflectional endings, it is not clear how we should deal with derivational morphology. For words such as *permit* or *segmentalizations* we would like

$$[\# \ \text{per} + \text{mit} \ \#]_{\text{Verb}}$$

and

$$[\#[[[[\text{segment}]_{\text{Noun}} + \text{al}]_{\text{Adj}} + \text{iz}]_{\text{Verb}} + \text{at} + \text{ion}]_{\text{Noun}} + s \ \#]_{\text{Noun}}$$

to be the inputs to the phonological component. Yet there is no known simple mechanism for explicitly generating the appropriate sequences of morphemes. Derivational morphology is one of the least understood areas of modern linguistics.)

We can now allow syntactic features to appear along with syntactic categorization in phonological rules. The following rule for Spanish states that the vowel immediately after the stem (i.e., the conjugation vowel) is stressed in imperfect tenses.

$$V \rightarrow [+ \text{stress}] / \quad \begin{matrix} X]_{\text{Verb}} + \underline{\quad} + \\ \begin{bmatrix} + \ \text{past} \\ - \ \text{perfect} \end{bmatrix} \end{matrix}$$

Diegueño, a Yuman language of southern California, has contrasts in vowel length. There is a class of verbs whose plural is formed by switching the length of the final stem vowel, so that if there is a short vowel in the singular there will be a long one in the plural, and vice versa.

Singular	Plural	
l̥ᵛap	l̥ᵛaːp	burn
ču:pu̥l	ču:puːl̥	boil
saːw	saw	eat

The Diegueño switching rule must make reference to verbs which are syntactically plural.

$$\begin{bmatrix} V \\ \alpha \text{ long} \end{bmatrix} \rightarrow [-\alpha \text{ long}]/\underline{\quad}C_0 \Big]_{\substack{\text{Verb} \\ [+\text{ plural}]}}$$

MORPHOLOGICAL FEATURES

Whereas syntactic features, such as [animate], [plural], [past], also function outside the phonological component of the grammar—in syntax and semantics—*morphological features* are uniquely required for phonological reasons. An example of a morphological feature was [+ 1 conjugation]. In languages with conjugational classes for verbs or with declensional classes for nouns and adjectives, these classes have no syntactic import. Their sole purpose is phonological, since inflectional endings may have different phonological shapes depending on the class. For example, in Spanish the present subjunctive marker is *e* for [+ 1 conjugation] and *a* for [− 1 conjugation], that is, the second and third conjugations.

A frequent type of vocabulary division is between *learned* and *nonlearned*. The English nonlearned vocabulary is basically Germanic in origin, whereas the learned is Romance and Greco-Latin. Certain phonological processes may be limited to one or the other of these types. For example, the alternations between *k* and *s* and between pairs of tense and lax vowels affect primarily the learned stratum. One also needs to distinguish between *foreign* and *native* words, as the former frequently exemplify special phonological behavior. In English, words such as *sphere*, *sphinx*, and *svelte* violate a morpheme structure condition that the second obstruent in initial obstruent clusters is a stop, and *svelte* may even violate the voicing constraints on such clusters. Hence, to account for certain phonological phenomena one may need to refer to features such as [− learned] or [+ foreign].

Exceptions

MINUS RULE FEATURES

Whenever a form meets all the requirements of a rule, then of course the rule applies to it and the form is changed in accordance with the rule. However, there are cases in which a form satisfies the conditions of a rule, but application of the rule would lead to the wrong result. On the other hand, if the rule did not apply, the form could be derived correctly. Any form which meets the conditions of a rule, but must not undergo it, is an *exception* to that rule.

In English there is a rule which laxes antepenultimate vowels.

$$V \rightarrow [- \text{ tense}]/\underline{\hspace{1cm}}C_0VC_0VC_0 \#$$

The rule for trisyllabic laxing accounts for the alternations exhibited in forms such as *divine, divinity; line, linear; serene, serenity; sane, sanity.* However, the morpheme *obese* is an exception to this rule. When this morpheme is combined with *-ity*, the antepenultimate vowel does not become lax—[ōwbīysitīy], not *[ōwbĕsitīy]. There is no explanation for this particular pronunciation, other than the word just being an exception to trisyllabic laxing.

Exceptions to rules can be indicated through feature notation. Among the specifications in the lexicon for the morpheme *obese* will be [− trisyllabic laxing rule]. (Alternatively, one could refer to rules by numbers—for example, [− rule 12]—with the number indicating the rule's position in the set of ordered rules. What is critical is that we be able to identify the rule in some way.) Specifications such as [− trisyllabic laxing rule] are known as *minus rule features*. The minus rule feature has the following interpretation for the morpheme *obese*: When one reaches the rule for trisyllabic laxing in applying the set of ordered rules in the derivation of *obesity*, that rule is to be skipped. In this way, the antepenultimate vowel of *obesity* will remain unaffected.

MINOR RULES

In English, there is a class of nouns ending in a voiceless fricative in which this fricative becomes voiced in the plural: *wife, wives; loaf, loaves; shelf, shelves; bath, baths; mouth, mouths; path, paths; house, houses.* We can account for these forms with the following rule:

$$[+ \text{ continuant}] \rightarrow [+ \text{ voiced}]/\underline{\hspace{1cm}}]_{\substack{\text{Noun} \\ [+ \text{ plural}]}}$$

However, not all nouns ending in one of these fricatives have voicing in the plural: *cliff, cliffs; proof, proofs; fife, fifes; birth, births; death, deaths; fourth, fourths; kiss, kisses; dose, doses; glass, glasses.* The plurals without voicing are in fact the "regular" cases, since English nouns generally do not change when the plural morpheme is added. Therefore, the rule which voices final fricatives must not apply to the majority of nouns.

Rules which only apply to a highly restricted group of items are called *minor rules*. In the lexicon we need to indicate which forms undergo a minor rule. One way to do this is to use *plus rule features*. The nouns *shelf, mouth, house*, and so on, contain among their lexical entries the specification [+ plural fricative voicing rule]. All other nouns would not contain this marking, and only items specified with the plus rule feature undergo the rule.

The alternations exhibited by many of the so-called irregular strong verbs of English are handled by minor rules: *bleed, bled; breed, bred; feed, fed; lead, led*; *meet, met*; or *swim, swam, swum*; *begin, began, begun*; *ring, rang, rung*; *sing, sang, sung*. Minor rules are needed to handle irregular forms, but only where there is "regularity" to the irregularities. Although the handful of irregular forms do not conform to the general pattern of the language, among themselves they follow their own pattern, and it is this "minor" pattern which is stated through a minor rule.

Why There Is Irregularity

Language is not perfect. There are irregular forms and rules which have exceptions. Irregularities are most often due to historical factors. Certain irregular inflectional forms—child, children; go, went; am, is, are—have a high frequency of occurrence and are learned early by the child. Such forms seem to resist various "regularizing" processes which have occurred in the history of the language. If there are enough forms of this type, and if they demonstrate patterning among themselves, then the synchronic language will accommodate the alternations by minor rules. On the other hand, if there is little or no patterning, the alternants would need to be listed separately in the lexicon, a procedure we have called suppletion. Sound changes in a language could stop before reaching all forms, or they might not affect all forms in the same way. Within a synchronic description there may then be morphemes which are exceptions to otherwise quite general rules. Words which are brought into the language after a sound change has run its course will not be affected by that change. This may lead to a division in the vocabulary, such as learned and nonlearned, or native and foreign. Because the phonology is essentially finite and a large number of words can be learned simply through rote, speakers can tolerate a good many exceptions and irregularities.

Natural Phonology

Some segments and processes are more *natural*, more expected, than others. Certain segment types are nearly universal; others are quite rare. Some segments are acquired early by the child; others do not develop until considerably later. There are also implications involving classes of segments—if a language has segments of one type, then it must also have segments of another type. Among the phonological processes are those which recur in diverse languages, while other processes have an extremely limited distribution. Here are a few examples of "naturalness."

1. Among three-vowel systems, *i*, *a*, and *u* are more natural than *i*, *æ*, and *o*.
2. Languages with front rounded vowels also have front unrounded and back rounded ones.
3. Languages which have nasalized vowels also have oral ones.
4. Among stops, *p*, *t*, and *k* are more natural than *p*, *t*, and *c*.
5. Palato-alveolar stops are rare, but palato-alveolar affricates are quite common.
6. In child language, fricatives emerge after stops.
7. Languages with affricates also have stops and fricatives.
8. Anterior consonants emerge before nonanterior ones.
9. Languages with voiced obstruents also have voiceless ones.
10. Languages with labialized consonants also have plain ones.
11. A rule which nasalizes vowels before nasal consonants is more natural than one which nasalizes vowels in word final position.
12. For obstruents to become voiceless in word final position is more expected than for obstruents to become voiced in that environment.

We would like to be able to characterize why some segments and processes are more natural or expected or normal than others. The framework we have established thus far does not show inherent differences in naturalness in any direct way. A matrix for p, t, and k is no simpler than one for p, t, and c, even when redundancies are indicated.

	p	t	k	p	t	c
Anterior +	⊕	−	⊕	+	−
Coronal −	+	⊖	−	+	⊕

Four nonredundant features need to be specified in both matrices. Worse yet, for the less natural three-stop system, c, which is less expected than t, requires fewer features for its nonredundant specification. Feature counting or symmetries in a matrix are not adequate for capturing the simplicity or naturalness of certain systems as opposed to others. What is needed is a way of marking the matrix to show the expectancy of stop systems containing p, t, and k, and the added complexity of three-stop systems of a different type or of systems containing stops in addtion to p, t, and k.

By the same token, a rule which voices obstruents in word final position is no more complex to write than the natural rule which devoices them in that environment.

$$[- \text{ sonorant}] \rightarrow [+ \text{ voiced}]/\underline{\hspace{1cm}} \#$$
$$[- \text{ sonorant}] \rightarrow [- \text{ voiced}]/\underline{\hspace{1cm}} \#$$

Here too we want some way of indicating that the first process is less natural, less to be expected, than the second.

Markedness

The naturalness of certain segments and phonological systems can be captured through the concept of *markedness*. The notion of markedness was developed first within the Prague school of linguistics and has recently been reintroduced by Chomsky and Halle. This framework allows two segments to be differentiated by considering one of them *unmarked* for a particular feature and the other *marked* for that feature. Important to the notion of markedness is the assumption that the unmarked member represents the less complex, the normal, or the expected state. For example, oral vowels are more normal than nasalized ones. The two classes are differentiated through their values for the feature [nasal]. If values for a feature are given as *marked* or *unmarked*, instead of + or −, and if the marked value is always the more complex one, then nasalized vowels would be marked for the feature nasal ([M nasal]), whereas oral vowels would be unmarked for this feature ([U nasal]). Since unmarked values are the expected situation, U markings will never contribute to the complexity of a segment. Hence, if two vowels, such as *a* and *ã*, differ only in nasality, the oral one will be evaluated as less costly.

SOME MARKEDNESS CONVENTIONS

We shall consider the markedness values applicable to stops for the consonant features [anterior] and [coronal]. Since the optimal consonant is articulated in the extreme forward part of the oral cavity, consonants which are [+ anterior] (labials and dentals) will be unmarked for this feature ([U anterior]), and consonants which are [− anterior] (palato-alveolars and velars) will be marked ([M anterior]). The feature [coronal] is handled differently for the anterior and the nonanterior consonants. For the former, an articulation with the blade of the tongue is more consonant-like. Consequently, dentals, which are [+ coronal], are [U coronal], whereas labials, which are [− coronal], are [M coronal]. For the nonanterior consonants, the body of the tongue is the normal articulator; hence, velars are more expected than palato-alveolars. Velars are [U coronal], and palato-alveolars are [M coronal].

	p	*t*	*c*	*k*
Anterior	U	U	M	M
Coronal	M	U	M	U

Among the stops, *t* is unmarked, *c* is the most highly marked, and *p* and *k* are intermediate in complexity. Other classes of consonants provide further evidence that dentals are unmarked for place of articulation. In languages which have only one fricative it is invariably *s*, and for those with one nasal it is usually *n*. Most languages have one or more liquids, often only the dentals. Language acquisition lends additional support to these markings. Jakobson has noted that anterior consonants are acquired before nonanterior ones. In terms of markedness, the first two consonants to emerge are those unmarked for [anterior]. The child's first task is to mark one of these for the feature [coronal], thereby opposing labials to dentals. Only after this first bifurcation does the child mark for [anterior]. The least complex situation would be to mark for [anterior] without also having to mark for [coronal]—the velars. Finally, the most complex case would be the marking of both features—the palato-alveolars.

The M's and U's in a matrix must ultimately be translated into +'s and −'s. The conversion is accomplished through a set of rules known as *universal marking conventions*, which are not determined separately for each language but are given *once for all* within the theory of natural or expected segment types.

The marking conventions applicable to stops for the features [anterior] and [coronal] are:

$$[U \text{ anterior}] \rightarrow [+ \text{ anterior}]$$
$$[M \text{ anterior}] \rightarrow [- \text{ anterior}]$$

$$[U \text{ coronal}] \rightarrow [\alpha \text{ coronal}]/\overline{[\alpha \text{ anterior}]}$$
$$[M \text{ coronal}] \rightarrow [- \alpha \text{ coronal}] \, [\alpha \text{ anterior}]$$

The rules occur in pairs. For every rule with a U to the left of the arrow, there is a corresponding rule with an M to the left and the opposite value to the right of the arrow. Futhermore, the marking conventions are ordered. Since α is a variable ranging over $+$ and $-$, and not over M and U, values for the feature [anterior] must be given before applying the marking conventions for the feature [coronal]. The value for the latter depends on that for the former: unmarked [coronal] has the same value as [anterior], whereas marked [coronal] has a value opposite to [anterior].

There are other examples in which values of one feature determine the expected values of another. Consider the feature [voiced]. The normal state for sonorants is voiced, whereas for obstruents it is voiceless. Consequently, [U voiced] is [+ voiced] for segments which are [+ sonorant], and [U voiced] is [- voiced] for segments which are [- sonorant]; conversely, [M voiced] is [- voiced] for segments which are [+ sonorant], and [M voiced] is [+ voiced] for segments which are [- sonorant].

$$U \text{ voiced} \rightarrow [\alpha \text{ voiced}]/\overline{[\alpha \text{ sonorant}]}$$
$$[M \text{ voiced}] \rightarrow [- \alpha \text{ voiced}]/\overline{[\alpha \text{ sonorant}]}$$

Again the universal marking conventions would assign values to the feature [sonorant] before assigning them to [voiced].

In other cases the universal marking conventions must take into consideration the environments in which segments occur. We noted for obstruents that the unmarked value for voicing is [- voiced]. However, it is often the case for languages which do not have contrasts between voiced and voiceless obstruents that obstruents are voiceless everywhere except in intervocalic position. This suggests that for single obstruents between vowels, [U voiced] should be interpreted as [+ voiced]. We also noted that dental consonants are unmarked for place of articulation. Consequently, *n* is the least marked of the nasals. However, the natural situation before consonants is for the nasal to be homorganic with that consonant. Therefore, for nasals preceding consonants the universal marking conventions should state that the values for [U anterior, U coronal] are those of the following consonant. A set of marking conventions for assigning $+$ and $-$ values will have to be sensitive to other feature values, both in the same segment and in adjacent segments.

Data from language change, language acquisition, and directions of implication are relevant to markedness. In language change, segments may become less marked. German voiced obstruents became voiceless in word final position. In language learning, more highly marked segments are generally acquired only after less marked ones have developed. French children acquire nasalized vowels after oral ones, which provides further evidence that nasalized vowels are more marked. Jakobson has shown that stops usually emerge before fricatives, and fricatives before affricates. By the same token, languages which have affricates also have stops and fricatives, but there are languages, such as French, with stops and fricatives but with no affricates. The directions of implication support the progression in acquisition. These observations suggest that, among the obstruents, stops are the least marked, while affricates are the most marked.

EXPLANATIONS FOR MARKEDNESS

We have said repeatedly that the least marked segments are those occurring in most languages, acquired early by the child, or resulting from language change. What we have not yet determined is why these particular segments are favored. It would be circular to argue that the reason certain segments are universal, emerge first with children, or are the product of linguistic change is because they are not highly marked. Consequently, marking conventions cannot be justified solely by these criteria. The conventions must ultimately be based on the *inherent complexity* of sound types.

For example, there are physiological explanations for the different treatment of voicing in sonorants and obstruents. It is natural, when in the speech mode, for the vocal cords to vibrate, as they do for the sonorants. However, when there is considerable constriction in the vocal tract, as for the obstruents, the flow of air through the glottis is impeded and the vocal cords would not normally vibrate. In order to produce voiced obstruents, additional adjustments must be made at the glottis; conversely, to produce voiceless sonorants, special effort is required to suppress the spontaneous voicing.

As a place of articulation, *palato-alveolar* is rare for stops, but quite common for affricates. Many languages, such as English, have only the palato-alveolar articulation for affricates. In these languages these palato-alveolars often function like the other stops. (For example, initial č is aspirated in English.) There is some physiological evidence to suggest that it is inherently more difficult, that is, much more muscular control is needed, to effect complete closure in the palato-alveolar region than in those regions where stops are commonly made.

The various secondary modifications impose additional articulatory gestures onto the primary articulation, so that the total articulation becomes more complex. In these cases the unmarked value of the secondary feature is

—, and the marked value is +. Thus, as we saw, [U nasal] is [− nasal] and [M nasal] is [+ nasal]. Similarly, [U aspirated] would be [− aspirated] and [M aspirated] would be [+ aspirated]; for consonants [U round] would be [− round] and [M round] would be [+ round], and so on.

Natural Rules

Just as there are natural or expected segment types, there are also natural phonological processes. For example, a rule which nasalizes vowels preceding nasal consonants is more expected than one nasalizing vowels in word final position; a rule which inserts a vowel between two consonants is more natural than one inserting a consonant in that environment; and a rule which makes obstruents voiceless in word final positon is more normal than one voicing them in that environment. How are we to recognize *natural rules*?

For some rules, the notation developed for rule writing will directly characterize those rules which are natural. Consider the two rules of assimilation, where vowels are nasalized before nasal consonants, and nasal consonants become homorganic to the following consonant.

$$V \rightarrow [+ \text{ nasal}]/\underline{\quad}\begin{bmatrix} C \\ + \text{ nasal} \end{bmatrix}$$

$$\begin{bmatrix} C \\ + \text{ nasal} \end{bmatrix} \rightarrow \begin{bmatrix} \alpha \text{ anterior} \\ \beta \text{ coronal} \end{bmatrix}/\underline{\quad}\begin{bmatrix} C \\ \alpha \text{ anterior} \\ \beta \text{ coronal} \end{bmatrix}$$

We can capture the naturalness of these rules by stating as a metatheoretical principle that we expect to find rules where a segment acquires feature values from a neighboring segment—that is, the feature specifications to the right of the arrow are identical to specifications in the environment. The following two rules, in which a vowel is nasalized at the end of a word and a nasal consonant becomes labial before coronal consonants, would not be natural according to the principle.

$$V \rightarrow [+ \text{ nasal}]/\underline{\quad} \#$$

$$\begin{bmatrix} C \\ + \text{ nasal} \end{bmatrix} \rightarrow \begin{bmatrix} + \text{ anterior} \\ - \text{ coronal} \end{bmatrix}/\underline{\quad}\begin{bmatrix} C \\ + \text{ coronal} \end{bmatrix}$$

The principle accommodates rules of assimilation and could perhaps be sharpened so as to include natural dissimilation processes. (We have oversimplified the problem; we would not want to value highly a rule which totally assimilates a consonant to a vowel. The metatheoretical principle needs refinement.)

There are many natural processes which do not involve assimilation and dissimilation. The following two rules state that obstruents are devoiced in final position, and that high and mid vowels are neutralized in unstressed position with high vowels appearing in this environment.

$$[- \text{ sonorant}] \rightarrow [- \text{ voiced}]/\underline{\quad} \#$$

$$\begin{bmatrix} V \\ - \text{ low} \\ - \text{ stress} \end{bmatrix} \rightarrow [+ \text{ high}]$$

For natural rules of neutralization, the resulting segment is the less marked of the segments entering into the neutralization. Thus, [− voiced] is the unmarked value for final obstruents, and, according to *Sound Pattern of English*, [+ high] is the unmarked value for nonlow vowels. We can establish as a second metatheoretical principle that we expect to find rules which make segments less marked. The following two rules, in which obstruents become voiced in final position, and high and mid unstressed vowels become mid, would be less normal.

$$[- \text{ sonorant}] \rightarrow [+ \text{ voiced}]/\underline{\quad} \#$$

$$\begin{bmatrix} V \\ - \text{ low} \\ - \text{ stress} \end{bmatrix} \rightarrow [- \text{ high}]$$

To say that a rule is less expected, or less natural, does not mean that it cannot occur as a phonological rule in some language, but rather that it does not enjoy wide favor in the phonologies of languages. In fact, in Yawelmani, long high and mid vowels are neutralized and the resulting vowels are mid.

The following two rules state that schwa is inserted between two final consonants, and that a consonant is deleted when the next word begins with a consonant.

$$\emptyset \rightarrow \text{ə}/C\underline{\quad}C \#$$

$$C \rightarrow \emptyset/\underline{\quad} \# C$$

We can state as a metatheoretical principle that we expect to find rules which lead to simpler syllable structure. Actually, this principle and the preceding one could be stated together: We expect to find rules which lead to less marked segments and sequences of segments. In a similar manner, we would hope to find metatheoretical principles governing natural rules of stress dynamics, strengthening, weakening, vowel shift, and so on.

NATURAL RULES VIS-À-VIS THE EVALUATION METRIC

There are many cases in which the formal notation reflects the complexity of a process. A rule which labializes consonants before any rounded vowel is more general than one which labializes consonants only before *u*.

$$C \rightarrow [+ \text{round}]/\underline{\quad}\begin{bmatrix} V \\ + \text{round} \end{bmatrix}$$

$$C \rightarrow [+ \text{round}]/\underline{\quad}\begin{bmatrix} V \\ + \text{high} \\ + \text{back} \\ + \text{round} \end{bmatrix}$$

The greater simplicity of the first rule is captured notationally by the fact that fewer features are required to specify its environment. There are other rules which formally are equal in complexity—such as the rule devoicing final obstruents versus a rule voicing them; yet one of the rules should be more "highly valued" than the other. For these cases we suggested some meta-theoretical principles for giving priority to the "natural" rule.

In French, final consonants are deleted before words beginning with a consonant or at the pause.

$$C \rightarrow \emptyset/\underline{\quad} \# \, C$$

$$C \rightarrow \emptyset/\underline{\quad} \# \, \|$$

These two rules are *structurally* similar, differing only in the final entity of the environment. Because of their similarity they can be collapsed with braces.

$$C \rightarrow \emptyset/\underline{\quad} \# \begin{Bmatrix} C \\ \| \end{Bmatrix}$$

So here is another example where the notation adequately reflects the simplicity (generality) of the process. This rule is a natural one, as the resulting sequences conform to preferred syllable structure. French has at least three other rules which perform this same function: (1) schwa is deleted before a word beginning with a vowel, (2) a sequence of vowel and nasal consonant is replaced by a nasalized vowel before another consonant or word boundary, and (3) *al* becomes *o* if followed by a morpheme beginning with a consonant—[lwayal] 'loyal', but [lwayote] 'loyalty' from | # lwayal + te # |.

$$\mathsf{ə} \rightarrow \emptyset/\underline{\quad} \# \, V$$

$$V\begin{bmatrix} C \\ + \text{nasal} \end{bmatrix}\begin{Bmatrix} C \\ \# \end{Bmatrix} \rightarrow \begin{bmatrix} 1 \\ + \text{nasal} \end{bmatrix} \emptyset \quad 3$$
$$\,1 \qquad\quad 2 \qquad\; 3$$

$$al \rightarrow o/\underline{\quad} + C$$

Although these four rules (the preceding three and the consonant deletion rule) essentially do the same thing—lead to CV alternation—the notation does not capture their *functional unity*. Given the present evaluation metric—feature counting—these four rules are no more highly valued than a set of four unrelated rules containing exactly the same number of feature specifications. Kisseberth has suggested that the theory must find a way to evaluate more highly those rules which "function" alike even though they are not formally (notationally) similar.

WHY NATURAL RULES ARE "NATURAL"

We noted that the markedness conventions must ultimately find their justification in the inherent complexities of segments, that is, physiological or psychological considerations will explain markedness. It seems likely that similar factors will provide the answer to why some rules are natural.

It has been suggested that rules of assimilation are to be explained through articulation. This observation is the classic explanation for assimilation, usually going under the rubric of "ease of articulation." Obviously, such notions need explicit characterization, which they have not always received in the past. However, some recent work in experimental phonetics suggests that the direction of the assimilation and the features which are assimilated can be explained in many cases as due to the coordination of different tongue muscles.

Psychological factors, particularly perception, provide a different sort of external explanation of naturalness. We have repeatedly mentioned maximum differentiation, a notion which accounts for the optimal opposition between consonants and vowels, and for *i*, *a*, and *u* as the basic three-vowel system. Many of the natural rules for preferred syllable structure and for neutralization can be explained as leading to optimal contrasts.

Relationship between Markedness and Natural Rules

That some phonological phenomena are more natural than others is by no means a recent observation; what is recent is the interest being taken in characterizing phonological naturalness. Universal marking conventions for segments illustrate one such attempt in this direction. A theory of natural rules is also needed to explain expected phonological processes. Natural segments and natural rules must be compatible. For example, the unmarked nasal is *n*, except when the nasal is followed by a consonant, in which case the unmarked value is homorganic with that consonant. As a phonological process it is also normal for nasals to become homorganic with a following consonant. Hence, context-sensitive universal marking conventions may be identical to natural rules of assimilation. Turning to the natural rules of preferred syllable structure, we would expect the syllable structures resulting from these rules to be compatible with the marking conventions for characterizing syllable structure within lexical items. If we consider the rules for neutralization, we see that they too have specific correlates in the marking conventions. Just as the latter stipulate that the optimal obstruent is voiceless, exactly the same condition obtains for word final obstruents which have undergone the neutralization (devoicing) rule.

The similarities between universal marking conventions and natural rules suggest that the underlying structure and the derived structure are governed by similar constraints, which we shall call *naturalness conditions.* Why should this be so? The naturalness conditions, as embodied in universal marking conventions, determine what kinds of segments are allowed in lexical representations and what sequential restrictions are imposed on them. These constraints may break down when morphemes are concatenated to form words and phrases, and where the phonological environments now go beyond individual morphemes. We can now view the phonological rules—one should emphasize natural phonological rules—as a second set of naturalness conditions whose function is to reimpose naturalness constraints on derived structures.

A Final Note

All languages have much in common in spite of their surface diversity. Notions such as markedness and natural rules are formal means whereby the linguist may account for such universal tendencies. However, in the end, the true explanations for naturalness are likely to be extralinguistic—physiological and/or psychological—so that phonology is not isolated from these other sciences. We will then understand better why certain traits are widespread, how children acquire the phonology of their language, the "feelings" or "intuitions" of speakers, and the direction of linguistic change.

The present-day language is the result of a long series of historical processes, many of which may continue to survive as phonological alternation. To explain these phenomena synchronically, we saw that there are different levels of analysis and rules systematically relating the levels. Because language has structure and follows "rules," the linguist, as an investigator of language, needs a notation for describing what he wants to talk about. But the notation, the formalism, the theory can only evolve from actual data. Consequently, we tried to look at data as a phonologist would and to discuss the criteria he brings to bear in carrying out an analysis.

I hope I have achieved my goal of showing how generative phonology works and how the generative phonologist works.

Bibliography

Items preceded by an asterisk are referred to in the text.
All other works are sources of data and analyses.

*CHOMSKY, N. and M. HALLE, *The sound pattern of English*. New York: Harper & Row, 1968.

*FROMKIN, V. A., "The non-anomalous nature of anomalous utterances," *Language* 47.1, 1971.

*FROMKIN, V. A., "Tone features and tone rules," *Working papers in phonetics* 21. U.C.L.A., 1971.

GLEASON, H. A., Jr., *Workbook in descriptive linguistics*. New York: Holt, Rinehart & Winston, 1955.

GRINDER, J. and S. H. ELGIN, *A guide to transformational grammar*. New York: Holt, Rinehart & Winston, 1973.

*HALLE, M., "Phonology in a generative grammar," *Word* 18.1, 1962; reprinted in *The structure of language: Readings in the philosophy of Language*, J. A. Fodor and J. J. Katz, eds. Englewood Cliffs, N. J.: Prentice-Hall, 1964.

HARRIS, J. W., *Spanish phonology*. Cambridge, Mass.: M.I.T. Press, 1969.

HOCKETT, C. F., *A manual of phonology* (International Journal of American Linguistics, Memoir 11). Baltimore: Waverly Press, 1955.

HYMAN, L., "How concrete is phonology?," *Language* 46.1, 1970.

*JAKOBSON, R., *Child language, asphasia, and phonological universals*. The Hague: Mouton, 1968.

*JAKOBSON, R. and M. HALLE, *Fundamentals of language*. The Hague: Mouton, 1956.

*KIPARSKY, P., "Linguistic universals and linguistic change," *Universals in linguistic theory*, E. Bach and R. T. Harms, eds. New York: Holt, Rinehart & Winston, 1968.

*KISSEBERTH, C., "On the functional unity of phonological rules," *Linguistic inquiry* 1.3, 1970.

KOUTSOUDAS, A., *Writing transformational grammars*. New York: McGraw-Hill, 1966.

*KURODA, S.-Y., *Yawelmani phonology*. Cambridge, Mass.: M.I.T. Press, 1967.

*LADEFOGED, P., *Preliminaries to linguistic phonetics*. Chicago: Univ. of Chicago Press, 1971.

LANGACKER, R. W., *Language and its structure*. New York: Harcourt, Brace & World, 1967.

LEE, C. Y. K., "Some phonological rules for consonant clusters in Korean," *Essays in commemoration of Dr. Tai Sik Synn's 60th birthday*. Taeger, Korea: Keimyung Christian College, 1969.

LIGHTNER, T. M., *Russian phonology*. Unpublished, 1967.

*NEWMAN, S., *Yokuts language of California* (Viking Fund Publications in Anthropology, No. 2). New York, 1944.

SCHACTER, P. and V. A. FROMKIN, *A phonology of Akan: Akuapem, Asante and Fante* (Working Papers in Phonetics, No. 9) U.C.L.A., 1968.

SCHANE, S. A., *French phonology and morphology*. Cambridge, Mass.: M.I.T. Press, 1968.

*STANLEY, R., "Redundancy rules in phonology," *Language* 43.1, 1967.

TRUBETZKOY, N. S., *Principles of phonology*. Berkeley: Univ. of California Press, 1969.

VENNEMANN, T., *German phonology*. Unpublished doctoral dissertation. U.C.L.A., 1968.

WALKER, D., "Diegueño plural formation," *Linguistic notes from La Jolla*, No. 4. La Jolla, California: U.C.S.D., 1970.

*WANG, W., "Phonological features of tone," *International journal of American linguistics* 33.2, 1967.

Index